The Secrets of the World's Seas

Atlantis, the Legend of the Lost Continent, and the Bermuda Triangle

Gabriel Glasman / Federico Puigdevall / Fernando López Trujillo

Cavendish Square

New York

This edition published in 2018 by Cavendish Square Publishing, LLC
243 5th Avenue, Suite 136, New York, NY 10016

First Edition

Website: cavendishsq.com

This publication represents the opinions and views of the author based on his or her personal experience, knowledge, and research. The information in this book serves as a general guide only. The author and publisher have used their best efforts in preparing this book and disclaim liability rising directly or indirectly from the use and application of this book.

All websites were available and accurate when this book was sent to press.

Cataloging-in-Publication Data

Names: Glasman, Gabriel. | Martínez, Javier Francisco. | López Trujillo, Fernando.
Title: The secrets of the world's seas/ Gabriel Glasman, Javier Francisco Martínez, and Fernando López Trujillo
Description: New York : Cavendish Square Publishing, 2018. | Series: The secrets of history | Includes bibliographical references and index.
Identifiers: ISBN 9781502632753 (library bound) | ISBN 9781502634429 (pbk.)
Subjects: LCSH: Geographical myths--Juvenile literature. | Atlantis (Legendary place)--Juvenile literature. | Bermuda Triangle--Juvenile literature.
Classification: LCC GR940.G53 2018 | DDC 398.23/4--dc23

Editorial Director: David McNamara
Editor: Erica Grove
Associate Art Director: Amy Greenan
Production Coordinator: Karol Szymczuk

Original Idea: Sol90 Publishing
Project Management: Nuria Cicero
Editorial Coordination: Diana Malizia
Editorial Team: Alberto Hernández, Virginia Iris Fernández, Mar Valls, Marta de la Serna, Sebastián Romeu. Maximiliano Ludueña, Carlos Bodyadjan, Doris Elsa Bustamante, Tania Domenicucci, Andrea Giacobone, Constanza Guariglia, Joaquín Hidalgo, Hernán López Winne.
Proofreaders: Marta Kordon, Edgardo D'Elio
Design: Fabián Cassan
Layout: Laura Ocampo, Carolina Berdiñas, Clara Miralles, Paola Fornasaro, Mariana Marx, Pablo Alarcón

The photographs in this book are used by permission and through the courtesy of: National Geographic Stock; Corbis Images; Getty Images; NASA; Gentileza Virgin y Jacques Collina Girard; AGE Fotostock; Topfoto, Granger, Other Images; L. Garlaschelli; Barry M. Schwortz Collection, STERA Inc.; Petaqui; Kris Simoens; Sacred Destinations Images; Dr. Leen Ritmeyer; Mitchell Library, State Library of New South Wales.

Printed in the United States of America

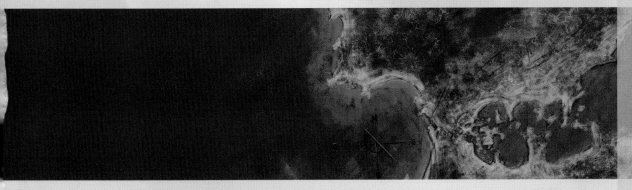

Can We Connect Thera with Atlantis?

Mankind has a collective memory – mythology. Through myths all cultures tell stories of a past, of an event, of a history, of something so astonishingly unusual that an account of it must be repeated, and remembered. Those stories are imbedded in every civilization as an integral part of the antiquity for that culture. It is an account of something huge that has shaped the current culture. And that account will, through time, be embellished, added to, expanded on then ornamented with whatever moral messages seem appropriate: it all happened because of an event that was good or bad that should be/not be repeated. Every culture, every story teller, takes their pick, and thus the account expands and grows with permanent embellishments, until fact and fiction merge and cannot be distinguished.

But for the myth to have immortality and a foundation for perseverance through time and cultures, the story must involve something so unusual, so big, so different, that it will likely not be repeated. Its foundation cannot be the commonplace happening. This was recognized by Plato over two thousand years ago: at the core of a myth is reality. And what better for this than a catastrophic natural event such as a giant volcanic eruption, huge earthquake, stunning tsunami, great flood, etc. Repeated occurrences for such events are geologically well beyond human lifetimes – perfect for a good story.

So, what greater natural event than a huge volcanic eruption, or series of eruptions, to seed a grand myth? And what greater myth in the western world than that of Atlantis? Plato's recording of a grand story some generations after it was first given to Solon, the Greek, by priests in Egypt, seems to speak of a huge, unexpected and brief, but intense disaster of untold proportions in the midst of a flourishing culture. Accounts of violent volcanism seem imbedded in myths from Hesiod (in *The Theogony* and the battle between the Titans and their offspring led by Zeus) and Apollonius (in *Jason and the Argonauts* as they sailed past the islands of Thera and Anaphi in the Aegean Sea). As with all stories, embellishments in their telling combined with translations from language to language blur reality. But that kernel of some reality possibly remains – something tremendous happened in the antiquity of the eastern Mediterranean region, and it seems related to volcanism and its concurrent events.

Consider what happened in the central Aegean Sea some 3,600 years, or so, ago during the Late Bronze Age – the core of a flourishing, wealthy, advanced society was suddenly and completely vaporized. Gone, disappeared, unexpectedly in a huge explosion. Its island foundation shattered to volcanic dust to be replaced by deep ocean. The surrounding region was devastated by earthquakes, tsunami, volcanic ash, climate change, and more. It was a stunning reversal to a peaceful world. This Minoan culture lived with seismic activity and had weathered numerous devastating earthquakes. They lived with the benefits of volcanism – productive soils, hot vents, mineral deposits – without realizing what a volcano was. Or what it could do.

Thus the Minoans were in for a surprise as the stuff of legends for ancient writers became their reality. We can only surmise that it is this specific eruption that led to these ancient accounts – there is no smoking gun or smoking volcano that can ever say that these legends describe the Late Bronze Age eruption of Thera. We can only infer and guess whether this ancient catastrophic affair was warped into intricate accounts of grandeur, wealth and societal decay. The suggestions and inferences will last as long as the legends persist. There can be no doubt that if Atlantis really was pre-eruption Thera, what a grand setting and city and culture is described, something of untold wealth and success. But equally, following Plato's description, what a startling decay into warlike tribes.

Floyd McCoy
PhD in Geological Sciences from the University of Harvard. professor of geology, geophysics, and oceanography at the University of Hawaii. He is the coeditor of the volume of scientific articles *Volcanic Hazards and Disasters in Human Antiquity*.

SANTORINI, GREECE
Before the volcanic eruption of
1600 BCE, Santorini had a circular
shape with a lake in the middle with
several small islets and a narrow
outlet to the sea. Many take this as
proof that Atlantis was there.

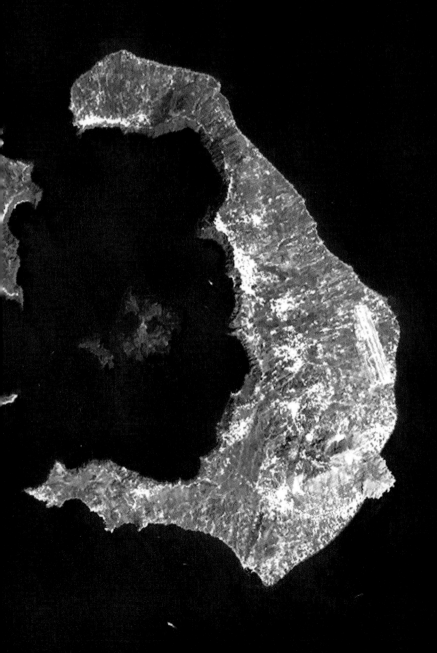

A Continent Submerged in Time

Atlantis is one of the greatest enigmas of civilization, not least for the uncertainty of whether it even existed. The first known reference to the city goes back to the fifth century BCE.

The possible existence of Atlantis raises controversy and has baffled the wise and gullible alike for centuries. While for some there is absolutely no doubt about the historical certainty of this ancient civilization, for others – including the majority of notable historians – it is pure fiction, created by Plato. The Hellenist historian Pierre Vidal-Naquet states that Plato would have written the discourses of *Timaeus* (and later, *Critias*) as radical critique of the port city of Athens. Vidal-Naquet's view is that Plato was not referring to a war between Athens and Atlantis, but rather a metaphorical war between two versions of Athens separated by a millennium of history.

THE VISION OF THE PHILOSOPHERS

The Greek philosopher dedicated a good portion of two of his dialogues to Atlantis. Given the sparse amount of ancient texts that have been preserved, two writings by the same author citing the same location, which include detailed descriptions, show that it is a theme that contemporaries would have seen as significant. If nothing else, it highlights the importance Plato attributed to this ancient civilization. It should be said that there is no other recorded mention of Atlantis until Plutarch resurrects the character of Solon of Athens, the formidable statesman and traveler, in his *Parallel Lives*. Sonkhis of Sais and Psenophis of Heliopolis are mentioned as Egyptian priests who instructed Solon in the history of Atlantis. Much later, in the fifth century, the Byzantine philosopher Proclus revived the character of Crantor of Sicily, who was said to have written an exegesis of Timaeus at the beginning of the third century BCE, in which he not only confirmed the veracity of Plato's tale, but even refers to a trip he made to Egypt where he examined stelae which confirmed Solon's account.

Additionally, Posidonius in the second century BCE, and Strabo a century later, speculated about the account, giving it merit. Their contemporary, Pliny the Elder, indicated in his *Natural History* that what Plato said about the Atlantic Ocean rising and flooding vast territories in the past was true. In Plato's dialogue, the account is attributed to Critias. He insists, several times, on highlighting the historical accuracy of the society and happenings in the narrative. Similarly

GREEK PILLARS
Legend places the city at the Pillars of Hercules, which no longer exist.

he strives to create a detailed and realistic description of the subject. The reference to Solon, who learned of the story of Atlantis from the mouths of Egyptian priests in the city of Sais, served to increase people's confidence that it had existed.

It is noteworthy that the story developed by Plato refers to the first contact between the Athenians and those postulated as "Atlanteans" as a failed violent conquest of a port city by the latter. The location must have been the polis of Attica, judging by when the event falls historically: no less than 9,000 years before Solon (circa 638 BCE–558 BCE). Let's do some calculations: six or seven hundred years previous, the Mycenaean civilization crumbled after a series of Dorian invasions. There was almost nothing left of what were the walls of Agamemnon's Mycenae. Although few doubted the exploits of Achilles and Odysseus in the Trojan war.

Some time before this era – approximately 3,500 years ago – the only activity recorded in the area with similar characteristics as those described regarding Atlantis were the Cretan invasions. Inhabitants of a great island, although nowhere near the enormous dimensions Critias attributed to Atlantis, the Cretans were a very developed and technologically advanced thalassocracy. The raids of this Minoan people against the blue backdrop of the Aegean Sea in the second

millennium BCE have given rise to many legends, constituting the majority of the content of Ancient Greek tradition. From a strictly chronological perspective, this saga is separated by a great distance from the era described in the Platonic dialogues, in fact millenia. It appears that the concept of chronology was not a strength of the ancients. Without attempting originality, it will suffice to mention that the first Western text considered to be the historical or at least mythical foundation of the story of Atlantis belongs to the

generation before Plato – to Herodotus of Halicarnassus, author of *The Histories*. Critias described an oblong island that could fit 3,000 × 2,000 stadiums, which would have been approximately 325 × 217 miles (523 × 349 kilometers). The island of Crete is perhaps 186 miles (299 km) long and 37 miles (60 km) at its widest part. This Minoan civilization has left records of its existence since the sixth century BCE. And there are numerous remains of its splendor which date back to the middle of the third millennium BCE. Archaeology has iden-

CRETE
Minoan culture achieved its highest splendor on the isle of Crete. It was there that the palace of Knossos was built, which contains decorative artifacts and pillars comparable to those described in the legends of Atlantis.

FRESCO
The minotaur is one of the most ancient of Greek legends, as well as a feared being in Minoan culture, which flourished in the Aegean sea long before Athens became the most famous polis of Classical Greece.

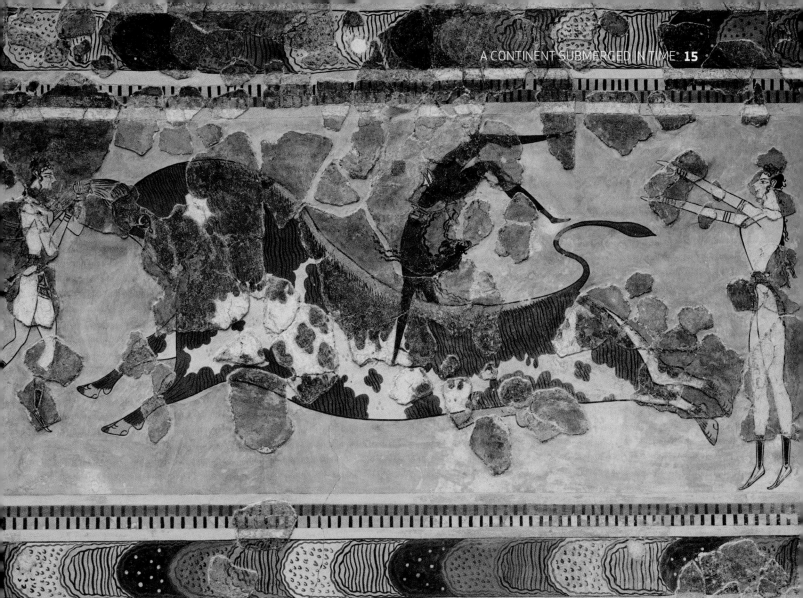

tified two catastrophes that this civilization suffered around the middle of the third and the end of the second centuries BCE. The latter could be identified as the Dorian invasion in the Eastern Mediterranean, with an additional maritime attack. And there is evidence of a tsunami, perhaps the result of a volcanic eruption on a nearby island.

Could Critias be referring to the Cretans in the dialogue transcribed by Plato? That is still a considerable chronological stretch. Some researchers offer other suggestions: if Solon received this information from the Egyptian priests, the dates would be linked to the Egyptian calendar, the accuracy of which is questionable. The objection seems insignificant. Are maritime battles conceivable in an area where the Neolithic revolution (10,000 BCE) had just recently occurred?

The statements of Critias continue to be discouragingly imprecise: "First of all, we must remember that nine thousand years have passed..." Nine thousand is not a very exact date. It seems more the product of speculation than of the counsel from those "manuscripts given by Solon to his great-grandfather, Dropidus," which Critias claimed to have in his possession.

Of course, there is not only the chronological problem. It turns out that the dialogue states that the immense island of Atlantis is "beyond the Pillars of Hercules." And they are located – according to all classical sources – someplace between Algeciras (southern Spain) and Ceuta (the tip of Africa). That is to say that Atlantis would have been in the Atlantic Ocean itself. This is not a given, although the name of the ocean comes from the supposed existence of that land.

Perhaps it would have been near the African coast, like the Canary islands. Is this volcanic archipelago perhaps even the remains of the island the ancients describe as the size of Libya? Could the Azores and Madeira be the remains of this island that sank into the sea? That is another hypothesis. Another angle to consider is that while it is true that the vast majority of mythical Greek references are not provable, for centuries the narrative of

Continued on page 18 ▶

Atlantis According to Plato

The Greek philosopher wrote of a marine city with a circular structure inhabited 9000 years ago. Its concentric channels, palaces, fountains, and gardens became a myth that continues to motivate scientific explorations in the seas and oceans of the world.

The City of Canals

Its primary characteristic was concentric rings of land separated from each other by waterways. The central island was occupied by the Acropolis, a racetrack, and the houses in which the most faithful troops resided.

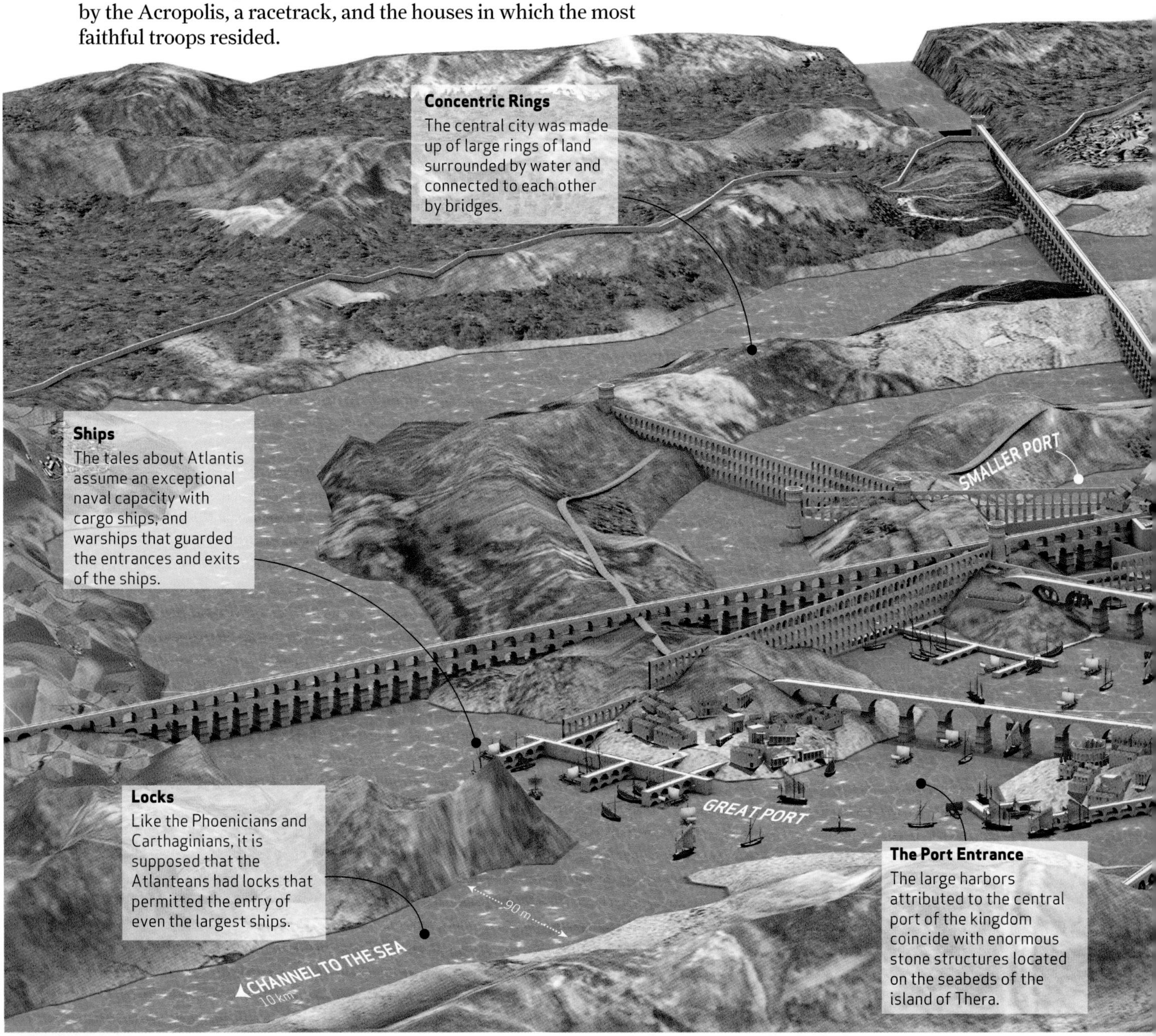

Concentric Rings
The central city was made up of large rings of land surrounded by water and connected to each other by bridges.

Ships
The tales about Atlantis assume an exceptional naval capacity with cargo ships, and warships that guarded the entrances and exits of the ships.

Locks
Like the Phoenicians and Carthaginians, it is supposed that the Atlanteans had locks that permitted the entry of even the largest ships.

SMALLER PORT

GREAT PORT

The Port Entrance
The large harbors attributed to the central port of the kingdom coincide with enormous stone structures located on the seabeds of the island of Thera.

CHANNEL TO THE SEA
10 km

90 m

enigmas

Did They Find the Mythical Circular City in Southern Spain?

Scientists of different disciplines discovered traces of a circular formation under the marshes of Doñana in Cadiz, Spain. A satellite image publicized by National Geographic suggests that Atlantis could have sunk here. Spanish geologist Juan Antonio Morales found cubical stone blocks at the mouth of the Guadalquivir River that could have been used when the sea level was 650 ft lower than the current level.

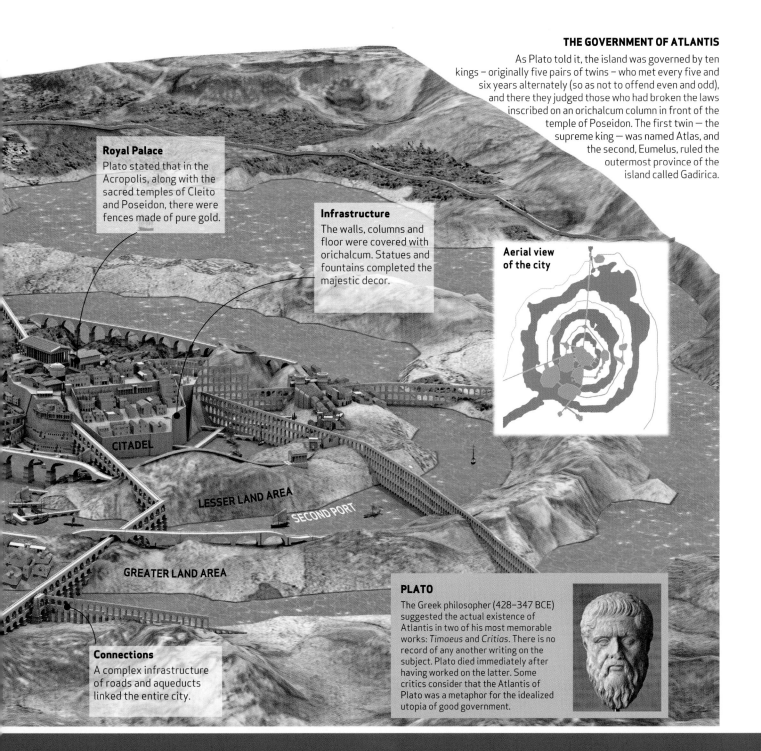

THE GOVERNMENT OF ATLANTIS
As Plato told it, the island was governed by ten kings – originally five pairs of twins – who met every five and six years alternately (so as not to offend even and odd), and there they judged those who had broken the laws inscribed on an orichalcum column in front of the temple of Poseidon. The first twin — the supreme king — was named Atlas, and the second, Eumelus, ruled the outermost province of the island called Gadirica.

Royal Palace
Plato stated that in the Acropolis, along with the sacred temples of Cleito and Poseidon, there were fences made of pure gold.

Infrastructure
The walls, columns and floor were covered with orichalcum. Statues and fountains completed the majestic decor.

Aerial view of the city

CITADEL

LESSER LAND AREA

SECOND PORT

GREATER LAND AREA

Connections
A complex infrastructure of roads and aqueducts linked the entire city.

PLATO
The Greek philosopher (428–347 BCE) suggested the actual existence of Atlantis in two of his most memorable works: *Timaeus* and *Critias*. There is no record of any another writing on the subject. Plato died immediately after having worked on the latter. Some critics consider that the Atlantis of Plato was a metaphor for the idealized utopia of good government.

Homer in the Iliad was likewise considered mythical until the amateur archaeologist Heinrich Schliemann discovered Troy in Turkey, near the modern city of Hissarlik, circa 1870. What is more, until the archaeologist Arthur Evans unearthed the city of Knossos in Crete in the twentieth century, Daedalus, the minotaur, and even king Minos were no more than legends. They are now considered elements of an important culture that scholars endeavor to write about in detail. Is this irrefutable proof that the myth of Atlantis is rooted in history? No, but it gives some weight to the idea of not writing it off as purely fantastical in origin.

Greek society in the era of Plato knew very little about its own origins and did not have records of the events which had occurred in the one or two thousand years previous. Critias himself mentioned this convincingly in the following cited dialogue: "Given the scarcity of sustenance for maintaining life, a scarcity that lasted for many generations, they and their children were occupied with satisfying their needs, and gave their spirit wholly to this one objective, and did not make efforts to record the events that took place. Scholarly study and recording history of ancient things came about with the advent of leisure in the cities, when a certain number of citizens, having secured the necessities of life, did not have to worry any more about what to eat."

THE MYTH OF ATLANTIS

The recorded history as it were of Atlantis is not long. It consists only of the Platonic dialogues, and the commentaries of his contemporaries and successors.

The history of the myth, nevertheless, is considerably more extensive. It is difficult to establish the precise timing of its appearance, although no doubt the discovery of the Americas by the Spanish awakened all manner of speculations on the idea. During that time, naming Atlantis as the place of origin of the Aztecs, Maya and Inca became a common literary speculation.

Perhaps the most extraordinary part of the legend is that speculation has not dwindled to this day. While the first historical mention we find of the island regards it as perverse and decadent, more recent versions created by the German romantics at the height of modernism present us with a lost paradise. The late awakening of several European nations at the end of the eighteenth century had much to do with this outlook. This is true of the great German romantic poets such as Novalis, and Italians such as Count Gian Rinaldo Carli (1720–1795). With the imposition of Christian dominion at the end of the Roman Empire, the Bible became almost the only source used to examine the beginnings of European humanity. This explains why the Italian and German nationalists sought Atlantic origins, to avoid being bound to Jewish descent.

In the nineteenth century, Jules Verne and Pierre Benoit added a new perspective, converting Atlantis into Utopia. It was a vision craved by a society experiencing the brutality of newly-born capitalism.

The rest is modern history. The last fifty years have seen substantial development and proliferation of science fiction. In response to considerable Soviet production of sci-fi in the 1970s, Western Europe and America generated a similar magnitude of the same. Riding the wave of this vigorous trend, the myth of Atlantis returned to the public forum, to the bookstore shelves and above all to the screen in documentaries and movies.

In recent years archaeological expeditions have also increased in number and in scope, both on land and in the sea, using submarines and new technologies for exploring the ocean floor, as well as using aerial and satellite photography. Considerable effort has been invested into shedding light on this mystery. Did Atlantis exist? We don't know. But

Spyridon Nikolaou Marinatos
1901–1974

One of the leading Greek archaeologists of the twentieth century. Director of the Heraklion Archaeological Museum in Crete. Directed numerous excavations in the region and in 1937 was named Director of the Greek Antiquities Service. As professor at the University of Athens, he oversaw excavations at several ancient Mycenaean sites including in the Peloponnese, as well as Thermopylae and Marathon, scenes of notable battles of the classical period. His most important discovery was the site of Akrotiri on the ancient isle of Thera, today's Santorini. Under thick layers of volcanic ash, Marinatos found a nearly intact city, which from then on was referred to as "the Greek Pompeii." Marinatos died while still involved in excavations on Akrotiri.

INFLUENCE On Crete, Marinatos established a strong professional relationship with Arthur Evans, the famous discoverer of the Palace of Knossos and the Minoan culture.

Paulino Zamarro
1947

Creator of an innovative theory on Atlantis, proposing that it was an island of approximately 2050 sq m located near the Cyclade islands in the Aegean Sea. He postulates that Atlantis disappeared due to a tsunami caused by the waters of the Atlantic entering the Mediterranean.

CONTROVERSY Zamarro objects to the theory of the opening of the Strait of Gibraltar in the Pleistocene age. However, carbon 14 dating in the Black Sea offers proof of this.

◀ *Continued from page 16*　　　　　　　*Continued on page 22* ▶

Pierre Vidal-Naquet
1930–2006

Distinguished intellectual of Jewish descent, born in Paris, France. After the Second World War, he graduated from the Faculty of Arts in Paris, taught at the Orleans School, the Lille Faculty of Arts, and the University of Lyon. A distinguished Ancient Greek historian, he collaborated with other prominent French historians such as Pierre Leveque, Michel Austin, and Jean Pierre Vernant. He wrote *Clisthéne l'Athenien* (1964), *Economies et sociétés en Grèce ancienne* (1972), *Myth and Tragedy in Ancient Greece* (1972) and *Travail et esclavage en Grèce ancienne* (1988).

CRITIC Vidal-Naquet questioned the attribution of existence to Atlantis based on the Platonic text in his work *The Atlantis Story: A Short History of Plato's Myth.*

"To Plato, all of history was a string of lies ..."

Jacques Collina-Girard
1956

Quaternary Geology expert at the French National Centre for Scientific Research and professor at the University of the Mediterranean at Aix-en-Provence. He proposes that Atlantis would have been an island on the current Spartel bank, across from the Moroccan coast. Based on data gathered by marine geographer Marc-André Gutscher, he states that an earthquake shook the area around 9,400 BCE, producing a tsunami that destroyed the islands. He considers that the end of the ice age caused the ocean to rise and that the rate of this rise later increased to 13 feet (3.9 meters) a century.

DISCOVERY In 2005, Marc-André Gutscher found sediments of around 13 in (33 cm) thick on the island of Spartel. This suggests that thousands of years ago it was hit by a tsunami.

Where Is Atlantis?

Different explorers, archaeologists, and historians have placed the "lost city" as having been located in various seas and on lands that were once underwater. There are three main theories: the first being that it was located on the Iberian Peninsula, the second placing it in the Atlantic Ocean, and the third in the Mediterranean or Aegean Sea.

THOSE WHO SUPPORT THE IBERIAN HYPOTHESIS

1 1592
Priest Juan de Maria was the first to link the Atlantis of Plato with Spain.

2 1673
José Pellicer de Ossau Salas and Tovar linked the Tartessians to the Atlanteans. They maintained that the island with the Temple of Cleito was located at the mouth of the Guadalquivir.

3 1801
Writer Fabre d'Olivet stated that Atlantis was found in the Western Mediterranean, between Spain and Morocco.

4 1803
Naturalist Jean Baptiste Bory de Saint-Vincent hypothesized that the Canaries are part of the island that disappeared.

5 1874
Geographer and archaeologist E.F. Berlioux identified the mythical island with the Atlas Mountains in Morocco and Gibraltar.

6 1911
Juan Fernández Amador de los Ríos proposed that Atlantis was Tartessos and the Iberian Peninsula.

7 1920
Geologist Aimé-Louis Rutot maintained that Atlantis was in Morocco.

8 1922
Archaeologist Adolf Schülten considered Atlantis to be Andalusia and the kingdom of the Tartessians.

9 1928
Elena Wishaw, Director of the Ancient Mediterranean Research Association, placed the submersed remnants of the capital of Atlantis off the coasts of Cadiz.

10 1984
Philologist Jorge María Ribero-Meneses points out connections between Tartessians, Tartars, and the Titans, and proposes that the Egyptians and Phoenicians came from Cantabria.

11 1994
Georgeos Díaz-Montexano maintained that the center of Atlantis was the south of Spain (Tartessos) and Morocco.

12 2001
Jacques Collina-Girard believed that Atlantis could be found at the mouth of the Strait of Gibraltar, on the island of Spartel.

Yucatán Coast (Mexico)

Bimini Islands (Bahamas)

Atlantic Oce

Lake Titicaca (Bolivia)

enigmas

Was the Island of Thera at the Center of Atlantis?

Several indications of this can be cited: a) Plato described palaces with several levels such as those discovered on the island of Thera; b) the plaster blocks shone in the sun "like silver" according to Timaeus; c) Santorini is in the middle of a volcano that exploded in the sixteenth century BCE and caused a tsunami that affected the entire area; d) the city had a supply of cold and hot water through pipes, and e) docks and channels like those described by Solon appear in the Akrotiri (Santorini) frescos.

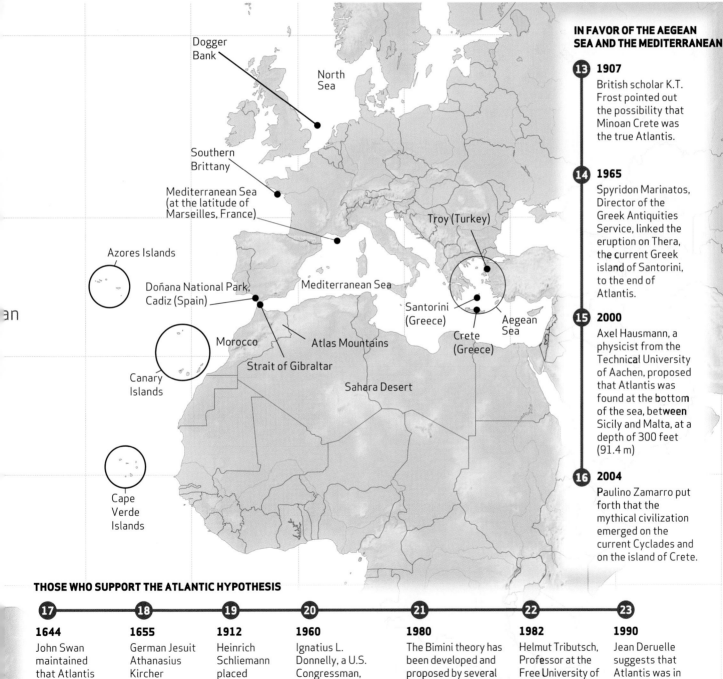

Dogger Bank

North Sea

Southern Brittany

Mediterranean Sea (at the latitude of Marseilles, France)

Azores Islands

Doñana National Park, Cadiz (Spain)

Mediterranean Sea

Troy (Turkey)

Santorini (Greece)

Crete (Greece)

Aegean Sea

Morocco

Atlas Mountains

Strait of Gibraltar

Canary Islands

Sahara Desert

Cape Verde Islands

IN FAVOR OF THE AEGEAN SEA AND THE MEDITERRANEAN

13 1907
British scholar K.T. Frost pointed out the possibility that Minoan Crete was the true Atlantis.

14 1965
Spyridon Marinatos, Director of the Greek Antiquities Service, linked the eruption on Thera, the current Greek island of Santorini, to the end of Atlantis.

15 2000
Axel Hausmann, a physicist from the Technical University of Aachen, proposed that Atlantis was found at the bottom of the sea, between Sicily and Malta, at a depth of 300 feet (91.4 m)

16 2004
Paulino Zamarro put forth that the mythical civilization emerged on the current Cyclades and on the island of Crete.

THOSE WHO SUPPORT THE ATLANTIC HYPOTHESIS

17 1644
John Swan maintained that Atlantis was found in the Atlantic.

18 1655
German Jesuit Athanasius Kircher stated that it was between Europe and America.

19 1912
Heinrich Schliemann placed Atlantis close to the Azores Islands and Madeira.

20 1960
Ignatius L. Donnelly, a U.S. Congressman, conducted research that placed Atlantis on the Azores Islands.

21 1980
The Bimini theory has been developed and proposed by several writers: J. Manson Valentine, Charles Berlitz, and Pierre Carnac.

22 1982
Helmut Tributsch, Professor at the Free University of Berlin, proposes the isle of Gavrinis, near Carnac in Brittany.

23 1990
Jean Deruelle suggests that Atlantis was in the North Sea on Dogger Bank.

Heirs of Atlas

Mythology states that Atlas was the first king of Atlantis, giving the island and surrounding ocean their inherited names. Later, the territory was divided into ten parts, with a king ruling each one. According to Plato, the foundation of good government for the Atlanteans was the dialogue between its kings, who met every five or six years alternately to reaffirm its laws. The meetings served as a collective control and, in the event justice was to be meted out, they held a ceremony dedicated to their highest divinity: Poseidon. The ceremony began with the hunting of a bull, without armor or iron weapons. Once captured, the bull was taken to the ten kings to be slaughtered at the foot of the pillar where the sacred laws and the terrible punishments for those who violated them were written. The bull blood was collected in a container to be thrown into the fire, after the kings sprinkled themselves with it in a purification rite. The ceremony continued with a renewed oath to keep the sacred laws and a personal promise made by each king, in the name of all their descendants, to enforce them for all the Altlanteans. Once the ritual was complete, the kings drank the bull's blood and left their cups in the sanctuary of Poseidon, and prepared for a new session of deliberation. Dressed in blue tunics, the kings sat on the ground in the ashes of the sacrificed bull and were judged by their peers with due justice served. Each sentence was recorded on a golden tablet, which was kept together with the clothing used for the occasion.

DIVINE PUNISHMENT
The legend of Atlas holding the Earth has several sources. One of them indicates that it was a punishment upon Atlas imposed by the gods.

The Perspective of a Writer

Jules Verne dedicates a chapter of his *20,000 Leagues Under the Sea* to Atlantis. The memoirs of Captain Nemo read: " ... led by the strangest destiny, I was treading underfoot the mountains of this continent, touching with my hand those ruins a thousand generations old and contemporary with the geological epochs. I was walking on the very spot where the contemporaries of the first man had walked. ... My heavy soles crushed the skeletons of animals from fantastic times, which the trees, now petrified, covered with their shade."

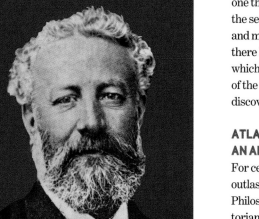

JULES VERNE
The French writer gave fame to the legend of Atlantis in the second half of the nineteenth century.

one thing we do know is that in the search for Atlantis, more and more lost cities, of which there had been no record, and which were not the purpose of the original research, were discovered.

ATLANTIS AS AN ARCHETYPE

For centuries, Atlantis has outlasted its physical existence. Philosophers, scientists, historians and a distinguished group of writers and opportunists have developed the most

Continued from page 18

diverse theories. The Platonic dialogues triggered a mystery that has lasted to this day. The innumerable and astonishing treasures that have been discovered underwater at all latitudes enhanced a search that combined historical and cultural knowledge with adventure. The persistent mystery of the lost city has also been a result of the moral lessons put forth in the Platonic text.

Many authors agree that the dialogues of Timeus and Critias are not about describing an actual civilization but rather about an ideal that humankind can achieve by following the right path of good government, mutual respect, and neighborly kindness. So, in Plato's writings, the wealth and greatness of Atlantis is portrayed as an example of the result of a harmonious relation between the gods, nature and humanity, achieving a social state of happiness and progress. Plato then develops the exceptional achievements of Atlantean society into a warning about the terrible consequences of violating the basic principles that made it what it was. When the kings became overly ambitious and sought war as the means of satisfying their appetite for power and material wealth, the great island gave way and was overcome by volcanoes, earthquakes and tidal waves. Even though, according to the Greek philosopher, the destruction of Atlantis seemed to be the punishment of the gods, the moral value continues to be valid.

CANARY ISLANDS
The volcanic makeup of the island of Tenerife features ancient craters such as those of the volcano Güimar. Remains of ancient maritime cultures, such as the Guanche, have been found in the area, which some link with the myth of Atlantis.

The Ruins of Akrotiri

The excavations made at Thera, currently Santorini, allow the reconstruction of an ancient society connected with the existence of Atlantis. Houses and several amphoras were found under a coating of volcanic residues. There are also beautiful frescos of images of daily life.

The Sea Festival

A fresco, 16 in (40 cm) high and 10 ft (3 m) long decorates the walls of a luxurious room in Akrotiri. It seems to describe a journey between two island cities. Below in the fresco, the city is seen before the catastrophe, with its red and white Atlantean stones and shining orichalcum; the far right resembles Amnissos, a port of Crete.

CONSERVATION The perfectly preserved condition of the site is because of the volcanic residues that have covered it since the second millennium BCE.

Who Built the City of the Atlanteans?

Plato wrote about the idyllic life in Atlantis, an empire established with the help of the Greek gods. Various authors later portrayed Atlantis as an exceptional kingdom with exemplary organization and a thriving economy.

Perhaps one of the most detailed representations of Atlantean life comes from Otto Muck, who based his imaginative description largely on the information provided by Plato. According to Munck, Atlantis was a true paradise blessed with a mild climate and rich soil for agrarian activities. The economy of Atlantis also benefited from mining. Their natural resources included deposits of copper, silver, gold, and orichalcum – a metal only second in value to gold according to the Greek philosopher. They also worked as stonemasons, mining rock for construction, said Plato, who highlighted the building of harbors and bridges of black, white and red stone. Population growth seems to have been proportional to economic growth, and some authors indicate that the population reached more than 50 million inhabitants, almost four times larger than the Egyptian civilization at the peak of its splendor.

WHAT THE CITY WAS LIKE

The wealth of the kingdom was displayed in its elegant architecture and in the magnificent mansions inhabited by the ruling classes. Much like in the great Greek metropolises, they adorned their parks and open areas with statues and monuments, and with crystalline water flowing from fountains. Engineering expertise allowed for sophisticated services to be provided to the masses, such as hot and cold water, which flowed into their homes and palaces. According to Plato, Poseidon himself had created two magnificent streams of water, of different temperatures, to flow from the sea into this land, for the use and benefit of the empire's inhabitants. The people also laid irrigation canals for crops, and for the purpose of conducting the streams of water to what they considered their sacred grove, dedicated to Poseidon. They also built numerous ponds and pools both outdoors as well as indoors, the latter being for public bathing during the winter. Men and women had separate baths. To avoid flooding, they constructed these baths in such a way that streams of water moved in the direction of the sea, via canals, making use of surprisingly practical engineering. Heavy cart traffic was supported by painstakingly designed roads, with the large population and their basic needs always in mind. Agriculture was assisted by an irrigation network that helped farmers cultivate the extensive arable land in their fertile valleys. Poseidon's grove was rich in all kinds of beautiful flora and tall trees. Numerous types of animals, including

Continued on page 28 ▶

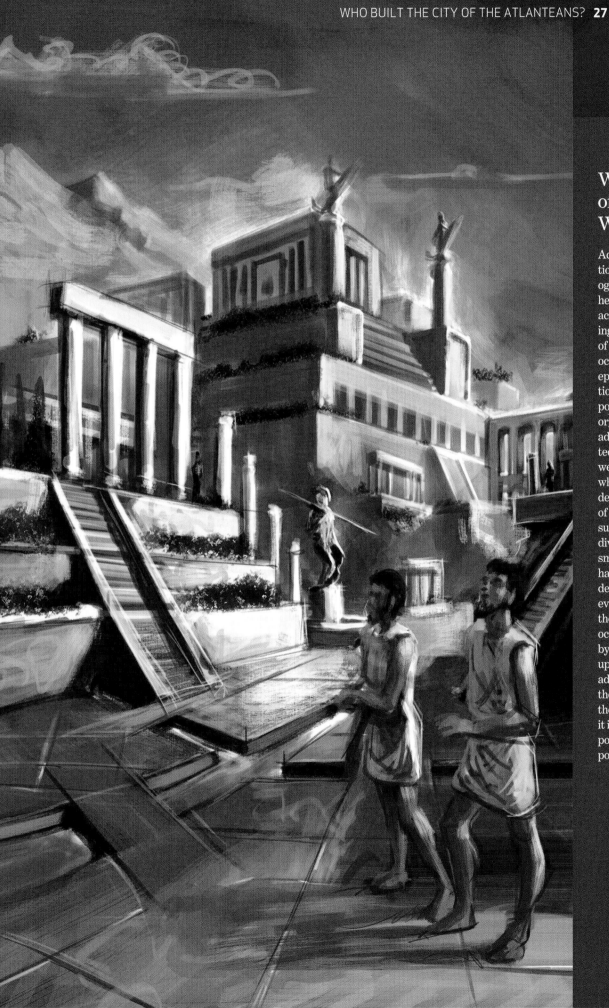

enigmas

Were the Citizens of Atlantis Warriors?

According to the descriptions of various Atlantologists, the society was heavily militarized. In fact, according to Plato's writings, the disappearance of the Atlantean society occurred during a battle of epic proportions. Descriptions of the civilization portray a tough military organization capable of administrating and protecting territories of great wealth and development, which inevitably had to be defended against the lusts of hostile kingdoms. It is supposed that Atlantis was divided into thousands of small districts; each district had five chariots for their defense force. Atlantis eventually possessed ten thousand chariots, each occupied and maintained by a crew of men, making up the kingdom's army. In addition, bearing in mind the capacity of its ports and the power of its economy, it is surmised that Atlantis possessed a considerably powerful naval fleet.

Atlantis: an Esoteric View

elephants, proliferated. The culture not only expressed its grandeur in its architecture, but also in its libraries and public teaching areas where the wisdom of the older members of society was venerated. Sculptures were found adorning the city throughout, particularly of Nereids riding dolphins. In the Acropolis, statues of the rulers and their spouses decorated enclosures covered with precious metals and marble. In addition, the sanctuary to the god of the waters was highly impressive, containing a monument of Poseidon holding the reins of a cart pulled by six winged horses.

POLITICAL ORGANIZATION

Atlantis as an empire consisted of an alliance of ten rulers who preserved territorial dependence within their coalition. The highest authority was these ten rulers, whose ruling power was guided by the use of a Constitution or code of peaceful coexistence accredited to Poseidon himself. Every five and six years alternately the rulers held a council, outlining common policies and affirming the mutual respect that was prevalent in their territories. Among their inviolable laws was one stating that they could never fight amongst themselves. Additionally, no ruler was entitled to take the life of one of their people without the consent of at least a majority of the other rulers.

Under the authority of each ruler was an extensive administrative and military bureaucracy that looked out for the well-being of each community, pro-tecting lands and fields and developing commercial activities and organizing the storage of goods. Considering their rate of economic growth and the numerous population, they must have had a well-maintained system of administration for internal and external commerce, which had to account for grain storage, animal breeding, and an outstanding chain of distribution.

The military establishment was of particular importance, ensuring the maintenance of a permanent security force (which some authors have estimated numbered almost a million) as well as the manufacture of chariots and adequate weapons for the purpose of defending the empire from enemy attacks. The peace enjoyed among the kingdoms of Atlantis seems to have been a reward earned through collective efforts, and there are no records of internal conflicts.

The rulers were considered to be direct descendants of the deities, and therefore their judgment and instruction were faithfully followed by their subjects. According to Plato's account, the rulers' virtue was boundless as long as they remained under the direct influence of the gods, but when the influence of the gods was superseded by earthly pleasures, the rulers digressed and fell into carnal idolatry. Apparently this particularly displeased Zeus, and he decided to punish the Atlanteans. The myth states that this decision was made immediately prior to the destruction of the civilization.

Although the majority of archaeologists and historians base their efforts to find Atlantis on the dialogues of Plato, in the nineteenth century there was a spate of philosophers who searched for the empire based on Biblical, Buddhist, Hindu, and esoteric sources. The biggest proponent of this trend was Helena Blavatsky, founder of the Theosophical Society. She maintained that Atlantis had been a continent filled with knowledge for a million years, and was inhabited by a race of giants with straight hair and red or yellow skin, an idea that had been communicated to her by a Tibetan monk.

Based on Theosophical ideas, many people began to believe in other mythical lost continents: Lemuria between India and Africa, Mu in the Pacific, and Hyperborea in the Arctic. The Egyptian, Scottish, Basque, Mayan, Canarian, and Polynesian peoples were considered by many to be reincarnations of the Atlantean line. The issue came up again during the nineteenth century, when various spiritualists said they had received messages from the thousand-year-old inhabitants of Atlantis. The esoteric Nazis also based their claim to Aryan purity on a supposed Atlantean descendancy. In light of the technological advances of the twentieth century, explorers put their hopes in numerous geological and satellite instruments to search for evidence of Atlantis.

◀ Continued from page 26

Helena Blavatsky
The Occult Rediscovery

After visiting the sacred sites of the world, the Russian philosopher and occultist Helena Blavatsky founded the Theosophical Society in New York in 1876. The discipline of Theosophy seeks divine truth by means of various religions. Drawing on sacred texts from Christianity, Tibetan Buddhism, and Hinduism, Madame Blavatsky proposed the existence of various lost continents, including Atlantis with its giant race. According to the founder of Theosophy, the Atlantean race was the fourth incarnation of the human spirit, on its journey from the origins of time to its final evolution. The Atlantean race supposedly would have inhabited a large continent reaching from the eastern part of North and South America to the borders of Europe and Africa, with a promontory north of the British Isles.

Blavatsky stated that she received this knowledge from a Tibetan monk, and had confirmed it through contact with spirits.

THEOSOPHY
Madame Blavatsky founded this discipline, which combines spiritualism and religion.

Theosophic Maps of Atlantis
The Great Transformations

1 **ATLANTIS IN ITS SPLENDOR**
According to Theosophy, Atlantean civilization reached its height a million years ago, when the continent reached from Iceland to Brazil, from the United States to Europe.

2 **WHAT REMAINED**
After four cataclysms, 80,000 years ago only the island of Poseidonis, which Plato referred to, remained. It sank in 9564 BCE.

MYSTIC BROACH
Initials of the Russian sprilualist with a swastika, an ouroboros, and a crown, all symbols of perfect immortality.

Edgar Cayce

A supposed mystical connection with the inhabitants of Atlantis was claimed by the healer Edgar Cayce, who told of a technologically advanced civilization that had used atomic energy 50,000 years ago in the Caribbean. Cayce, who diagnosed illnesses while under hypnosis, and worked with past life regression, announced that Atlantis would reappear off the California coast in 1968/69. His prediction apparently did not come true.

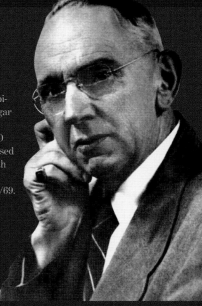

CLAIRVOYANT
The North American psychic Edgar Cayce proposed that Atlantis was in the Bahamas.

Was Tartessos the Successor of Atlantis?

Ten million years ago, the territories of Morocco and Spain were united. At the mouth of the Guadalquivir River, now submerged beneath the ocean, was the center of a culture supposedly founded by survivors of Atlantis.

Though there is a common certainty in the two theories about the location of Atlantis, they differ on how the empire was founded. Those who are inclined to identify Atlantis with the reign of the Tartessians, or at least recognize them as survivors of Atlantis, describe a different geography for the Iberian peninsula 11,500 years ago. At that time, the Atlantic and the Mediterranean were 325 feet shallower. You could walk from Cadiz to Tangiers. Spain and Libya were united by an archipelago covering approximately 19.03 acres (77,000 sq m). However, the end of the Ice Age brought a steady increase in the ocean's depth, which meant less exposed land. The French researcher Jacques Collina-Girard states that the study of coral in the area shows that after a mil-lennium of ice slowly melting, there was a sudden increase in sea level, "which rose at a rate of 6.5 feet per century, although sometimes the waters rose at a rate of 13 feet or more."

Around 9000 BCE, the seas rose swiftly, and Atlantis disappeared forever beneath the waves. Collina-Girard asserts that a submerged island found 150 feet beneath the surface near Cap Spartel in Morocco belongs to the lost empire of Atlantis.

THE ISTHMUS

If the Strait of Gibraltar were blocked, it is probable that the waters of the Mediterranean would be even shallower than those of the Atlantic. The Spaniard professor Paulino Zamarro believes that he can prove that the isthmus of Gibraltar ruptured around 7500 BCE. The waters of the Atlantic Ocean then rushed violently into the Mediterra-nean. On its eastern edge, the flood forced its way through the strait of Dardanelles, inundating the Black Sea, a freshwater lake that then became a saltwater sea. However, Zamarro believes, as do Greek researchers, that the island of Atlantis is actually found in the Aegean Sea, near the Cyclades at the southern tip of Greece. The violent flood would have been responsible for a surge that destroyed the coasts and islands of the Aegean, wiping out the ancestors of the Mino-an culture.

For its part, philology pro-vides some possible evidence in favor of the Tartessians. The word "Atlas" means "intermediate area" in the Iberian, Greek, and Berber languages. Thus, "Atlantis" means "city of the interme-diate area." And Tharsis, the presumed capital of the Tart-essians, has the same mean-ing in that language.

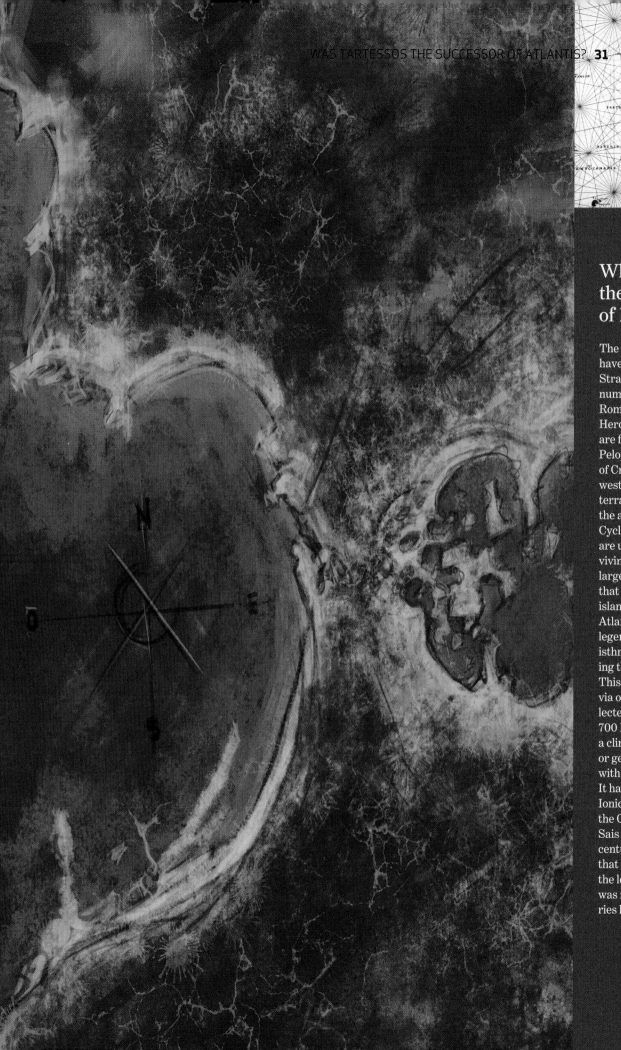

Where Were the Pillars of Hercules?

The Pillars of Hercules have been placed in the Strait of Gibraltar by numerous Greek and Roman authors. However, Herodotus insists that they are found between the Peloponnese and the island of Crete, and not on the far western edge of the Mediterranean. This is precisely the area occupied by the Cyclades Islands, which are undoubtedly the surviving remnants of much larger islands. It is possible that Plato referred to these islands when describing Atlantis. According to legend, Hercules broke the isthmus of Gibraltar, flooding the Mediterranean. This tale was transmitted via oral tradition until collected by Hesiod around 700 BCE, and reinterprets a climatic phenomenon or geological disturbance with a mythical tone. It has been proven that Ionic mercenaries from the Cyclades settled in Sais (Egypt) in the eighth century BCE. Is it possible that they took with them the legend of Atlantis that was recovered two centuries later by Solon?

Did a Tsunami Submerge Atlantis?

The Mediterranean Sea was once solid ground before geological movements transformed it. One of the most widespread theories about the disappearance of Atlantis is based on this scientific data.

The myth of flooding as the cause of the disappearance of great civilizations has accompanied the human culture since the oldest times. In fact, it is found in writings as dissimilar and distant as the Bible and the Popol Vuh – a telling of the creation of the world by the Maya-Quiché culture.

If, as put forth by various specialists, Atlantis is submerged in the Atlantic Ocean or the Mediterranean Sea, whose depths were very unstable for thousands of years, there is a plausibility to associating the end of Atlantis with a large flood of water covering the earth.

MYSTERIES FROM THE SEA

Geological science has determined that the floor of the Atlantic Ocean, in a wide band that extends from the Caribbean to Iceland, has been radically changed by the proliferation of volcanic activity. In the distant past, eruptions followed by tsunamis and the submerging of islands, as well as the emergence of others, have been recorded in the so-called "oceanic seismic belt" (the Mid-Atlantic Ridge). Similar features extend to parts of the Brazilian and Spanish coasts in a far-reaching arc.

The presumption that Atlantis ended its days in a volcanically-caused cataclysm was credited by geologists and volcanologists after analyzing samples taken from the ocean floor near the Azores Islands, where the projections and valleys far more closely resemble the earth's surface than they do in other parts of the sea floor. Samples of rock taken from the depths show, in addition, that they were covered in basaltic lava with properties characteristic of hardening above the water, which indicates that they were part of the earth's surface that disappeared below water. This theory was upheld by French geologist Pierre-Marie Termier, who stressed the possibility of a flooding of the earth's surface after it cooled, which is concordant with the process of vitrification found in the samples. If it had been otherwise, he has maintained, the samples would have presented a crystalline appearance.

The exsistence of a double plateau at the base of the Azores raises the idea that they emerged from a surface that was previously submerged in stages, which coincides with the account of a cataclysm allowing Atlantis to be abandoned in an orderly fashion. Thus science and myth align in such a way that the mystery of Atlantis continues to enthrall many.

Was a Large Meteorite Responsible?

Among the various explanations for the disappearance of Atlantis, one referring to a possible cause of an extraterrestrial nature stands out. Otto Muck is one of the geologists who supports this hypothesis. He suggests that the marine cataclysm that submerged the Atlantean civilization was the product of a falling meteor of immense proportions, which, when striking the waters of the Atlantic Ocean, caused the sea bed to fracture, resulting in a tsunami that wiped out everything, even at great distances from the impact. Evidence of similar phenomena is provided by the large number of craters caused by falling meteors in some areas of the Carolinas in the United States. According to Muck, it is possible that such craters were caused by debris from a larger meteor that broke off and finally fell to Earth. The mother meteor could then have fallen into the water, some 550 miles (885 km) from the coast.

The Inheritance of a Culture

At the beginning of the twentieth century, the ruins of the Palace of Knossos were discovered in Crete. The find allowed the Minoan culture, ancestor to Classic Greek and Mycenaean culture, to be reconstructed. The Minoan culture has been associated with possible Atlantean origins by many researchers.

Sculptures

Minoan art has not left us large works, but has given us numerous small statuettes, which it is believed was one of its significant characteristics. In general, the dimensions of these objects range from 1 to 8 in, and their motifs generally express a certain naturalism within the civilization, showing chiefly animals and people of both genders. According to the period to which the Minoan culture pertains, the preferred materials for use in statues were gold, ivory and bronze, although pieces in fired clay, nacre, glazed ceramic and marble were also found. Sometimes various materials were combined in a single object. The use of animal images such as snakes, donkeys and goats is directly related to religious practice and worship. Images of this nature were found in large quantities in sanctuaries and caves. The figure of the bull is particularly prominent, recurring in Cretan statues and frescos, and revered as a representation of masculine fertility.

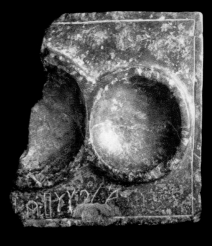

OFFERING TABLE
Found in Knossos, made of black ceramic. Its inscriptions in Linear A, a Cretan writing characteristic of official palatial and religious ceremonies, stand out.

PAINTINGS
The numerous frescos found in the Palace of Knossos constitute the compound's outstanding decor. Vividly colored, they were found on the palace's main walls and columns. Their lines, chromatic shades, and motifs such as birds, flowers, fish, and scenes from daily life, are noticeably similar to findings from the 1960s on the island of Akrotiri. This enhances the idea of an intimate relationship between both cultures, which have been indicated as descendants of the Atlanteans.

The Crete King's Palace

In 1900, British archaeologist Arthur Evans discovered the ruins of the palace of Crete, which was identified with the legendary labyrinth of the Minotaur and the Crete King's palace Knossos. The characteristics of the construction itself and the objects found there revealed the existence of a pre-Hellenic culture that developed between 3,000 and 1,400 BCE.

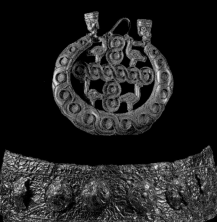

PHAISTOS DISK
Minoan goldsmithing produced gold pieces, medallions, and amulets with engraved inscriptions. This particular disk shows a type of linear writing not yet deciphered, which is read along the spiral.

GOLDSMITHING
Necklaces, pendants, and bracelets were made primarily in gold. The inscriptions found on some of these pieces were the names of those who wore them.

VESSELS
Vessels were made of fired clay and ceramic, and their sizes and shapes were related to their intended use, from collecting and holding water and oil to storing seeds and grains.

SHAPES AND MOTIFS
Shapes included tall vessels with wide mouths and small bases, with a pronounced width in the middle. Motifs alternated straight lines with curves, using designs of extended leaves and stylized waves.

SNAKE GODDESS
Made of glazed ceramic, one of the best-known pieces is of a woman wearing the dress and adornments of a goddess or priestess. She is thought to be the representation of feminine fertility.

Traces of the Atlanteans?

The volcanoes of the Canary Islands show ancient signs of activity, earthquakes, and spiral etching. In a triangle of the Atlantic Ocean, others search for ruins of an antediluvian center common to Egypt and America.

In the Middle Ages, a theory was proposed suggesting that the Canaries, Madeira and the Azores were the vertices of a triangular island located east of the Strait of Gibraltar. The conquest of the Americas led the Spaniards to a new hypothesis: the Antilles were another vertex of the submerged continent of Atlantis. In the nineteenth century, literature contributed to the discussion. In *Twenty Thousand Leagues Under the Sea*, Jules Verne imagines a descent to the depths to see the submerged empire of Atlantis. He tells us: "A day and a night was enough for the annihilation of Atlantis, whose highest peaks, Madeira, the Azores, the Canaries and the Islands of Cape Verde, remain visible." Tenerife is an almost perfect cone presided over by Mt. Teide, rising from the island's center. The entire island is the mountain's slopes,

that drop off into the ocean and which many geologists and volcanologists believe constitute the remnants of a tremendous volcanic explosion accompanied by a colossal earthquake. Clay remains found 24,000 feet (7,315 m) below the ocean's surface gave new life to the theory that the earth's surface was flooded, covering temples, palaces and their relics for eternity. The discovery suggests that these Atlantic islands may be the highest peaks of the lost continent. Temples and palaces would have remained covered by water.

THE SUPPOSITIONS OF A CONGRESSMAN

A series of relics found in the Canary Islands were dated to the fifth century BCE and link the natives of these islands to the solar worship cultures common to the Cretans and Phoenicians. The spiral etchings, much older

than those of the Canaanites, were associated with the design of the city of Atlantis as described in the Dialogues of Plato. In the mid-nineteenth century, the legend of Atlantis fascinated the people of that time and caused them to predict that it would soon be found. U.S. congressman Ignatius L. Donnelly wrote *The Antediluvian World* in 1883, in which he speculated that the location of Atlantis was in the center of the homonymous ocean. The similarities found between the cultures of ancient Egypt and the Mesoamerican civilizations showed, according to him, a common origin, which he stated to be a central source in the Atlantic within the triangle formed by Madeira, the Azores and the Canaries. Donnelly captivated his contemporaries, who launched a search for remnants of the ancient civilization in America, northwest Africa, and the Iberian Peninsula.

enigmas

The Mysterious Island of St. Brendan

A popular legend in the Canaries tells of an island called St. Brendan that appears and disappears in the fog. Those who have seen it place it to the west, between La Palma, La Gomera and Hierro, though there is no scientific proof of its existence. The only evidence of its existence is its presence on the world map made by Jaques de Vitry, a cartographer who described the island in the thirteenth century. Three centuries later, there were persistent efforts to find the island and include it on maps. In fact, Phillip II entrusted this task to royal cartographer Leonardo Torriani, who then included the island in the kingdom's navigational maps. However, to this day no one has been able to find the island, which continues to confound and experienced alike.

Underwater Exploration

There are two ways to search for archaeological evidence underwater: diving and remote searching by means of sensors. Mapping the ocean floor is an important aspect of exploration and facilitates the detection of anomalies attributed to human construction. Manned and robotic vehicles are used.

The Bahamas Ruins

In 1968, North American divers headed by zoologist Joseph Manson Valentine found a wall of blocks some 16 feet (4.9 m) underwater near Bimini Island, a part of the Bahamian archipelago. They attributed the arrangement of the rocks to artificial construction, which may correspond to Atlantis. Radiocarbon dating by the University of Miami estimated that the blocks were 3,500 years old. Other studies dated the stones at 15,000 years old. Various geologists assert that the Bimini wall is in reality a natural formation. The psychic Edgar Cayce, by means of a "sixth sense," put forth that the empire of Atlantis was submerged between the Gulf of Mexico and the Mediterranean. Meanwhile, the majority of scientists concur that the Bimini rocks could well be beach rocks fractured along relatively straight lines with right angles.

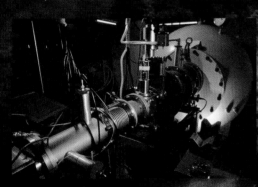

LINEAR ACCELERATOR
This machine can count the carbon atoms present in an organic sample to determine its age.

The Most-Used Instruments

Marine archaeologists use different technologies to search for evidence of ancient cultures, whether objects, sunken ships or stone blocks. Small but sophisticated, these devices function as extensions of the human senses.

SONAR
It is used to discover underwater anomalies indicating possible human construction. There is lateral sweep sonar, single beam sonar, and multiple beam sonar. Those that use beams to cause an echo allow maps to be created.

SENSORS
Electronic devices that measure temperature, movement, and even the presence of chemical elements.

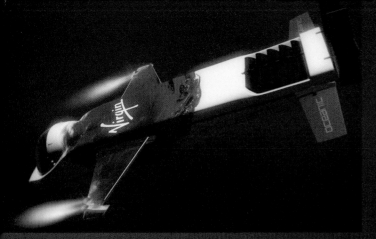

The Flying Submarine

The first manned vehicle capable of reaching the deepest parts of the ocean (4–7 mi [(6-11 km)] below the surface) was launched in 2011 by the company Virgin Oceanic. The mini-sub, 16 ft (4.8 m) long by 10 ft (3 m) wide, has a cockpit and wings similar to a plane, which allows it to navigate quickly.

Underwater vehicles

To reach great depths, different types of manned and unmanned robots are used.

DIVING
The use of sophisticated rebreathing equipment gives underwater archaeologists more time underwater, allowing them to dive to a depth of 130 ft (39 m) or more up to eight times, thanks to a backpack tank that pumps oxygen without releasing bubbles.

OBSERVATION
Upon approaching the rocky sediment, divers can determine whether it is of marine origin or is from the surface.

PIONEER
The famous Woods Hole oceanography institute in the United States developed the mini-sub Alvin, capable of reaching depths of 3 mi (4.8 km) for 6 hours. It was relaunched in 2012 with new instruments.

ROV
Different types of Remotely Operated Vehicles (ROVs) have been built that are operated via fiber optic cables. For example, the North American robots Medea and Jason can descend 6 mi (4.8 km) and operate for 21 continuous hours. The French government also has an ROV.

AUV
The most advanced robots are completely autonomous (Autonomous Underwater Vehicles and are guided by computer programs and sensors of all types. For example, SeaBED has been inspecting the Aegean Sea since 2005 searching for sunken ships around Santorini and Crete.

MAGNETOMETER
Measures magnetic fields emitted by rocks, metal, and buried objects.

CAMERAS
Some robots have devices to obtain high-resolution images, whether through optic photography or digital images and high-definition video.
To reach great depths, the cameras are placed on platforms.

ROBOTIC ARM
Some vehicles are equipped with robotic arms, used to manipulate objects and sediments.

GPS SYSTEM AND TRANSPONDERS
Although Global Positioning System (GPS) signals do not penetrate the sea, there are transponders that can send the location of a robot explorer to ships.
There are also undersea WIFI systems.

Did They Have Modern Technologies?

An increasing suspicion is shaking up prehistoric experts. Ancient traces of advanced technical development are consistently appearing, which science has thus far classified as being from a much later period.

An example is the famous Baghdad pillar, which could be five thousand years old. The same technology needed to hoist stones for the oldest Egyptian pyramids was probably achieved when they raised the obelisks in the first millennium BCE, but it is hard to imagine that it was possible to lift them three thousand years earlier. It is logical that the lack of answers to these questions causes great speculation. Amongst the most well-known speculations, and one which stands out over the rest, is that the citizens of Atlantis possessed object levitation technology. It seems that their mastery and channeling of various energies permitted them to lift objects regardless of their mass or weight. Additionally, it is necessary to mention a rumor that may never be silenced. Did the Egyptians have a way of softening the stones and then hardening them, in order to be able to make them exactly the right shape for their specific location? A scholar in Cuzco has arrived on the scene who recovered information regarding an ancient tradition to produce the substance used in construction in Machu Picchu and Saksaywaman. Shortly afterward, on Sehel Island in the Nile, the Famine Stele was found and deciphered, with a formula for preparing a similar substance. The connection between the two continents through a superior and older culture seemed evident.

THE POPOL VUH

The search for traces of Atlantis continued in America. It was associated with the Fourth Race named in the Maya book Popol Vuh. They spoke of incandescent lamps which lit their palaces. It is believed that Tesla, the famous inventor, knew of this technology, and worked to improve Edison's light bulb and design an energy production and distribution system; it did not interest the growing monopoly who judged it to be cheap and not businessworthy. The "illuminations" that came through mediums at the end of the nineteenth and the beginning of the twentieth century, via Madame Helena Blavatsky and Edgar Cayce, describing the place where the Bimini constructions were later found, must also be similarly rejected. The Atlantean temple of Inkaliclon, a gigantic pyramid, was described as being made of white granite, built in an electromagnetic vortex, over which a crystal cube had been levitated. A soft white light was said to have streamed from it, which disintegrated any object that entered its field.

Were they able to soften stone?

How were they able to lift rocks to the altitude at which Machu Picchu was built? According to the priest Jorge Lira, scholar of Quechua culture, the gods had given two presents to the Andean peoples for construction: the coca leaf, to relieve their great efforts, and the formula of a substance to make stone into a soft dough, which they could mold easily. The main ingredient for this substance seems to be from a bush, the "Jotcha," with which experiments have been conducted where they managed to soften solid rock to the point of almost liquefying it. They did not manage to make it hard again, so the experiment was considered a failure. Also, Dr. Joseph Davidovits, an expert in geopolymer material, tested out a formula taken from the Famine Stele, around 2 miles (3.2 km) from the Aswan Dam, with results that were similar to those obtained by the Peruvian: he liquidized the stone, but could not return it to its solid state. Nevertheless, the discovery of hair and other objects within the gigantic stones serves as proof to many that such a technique must have existed.

THE BIMINI ROAD
This odd underwater rock formation
nearly 0.6 mi (.96 km) in length
is located to the north of Bimini
Island, in the Bahamas. Many see
in it the structure of a road or wall,
vestiges of a lost city.

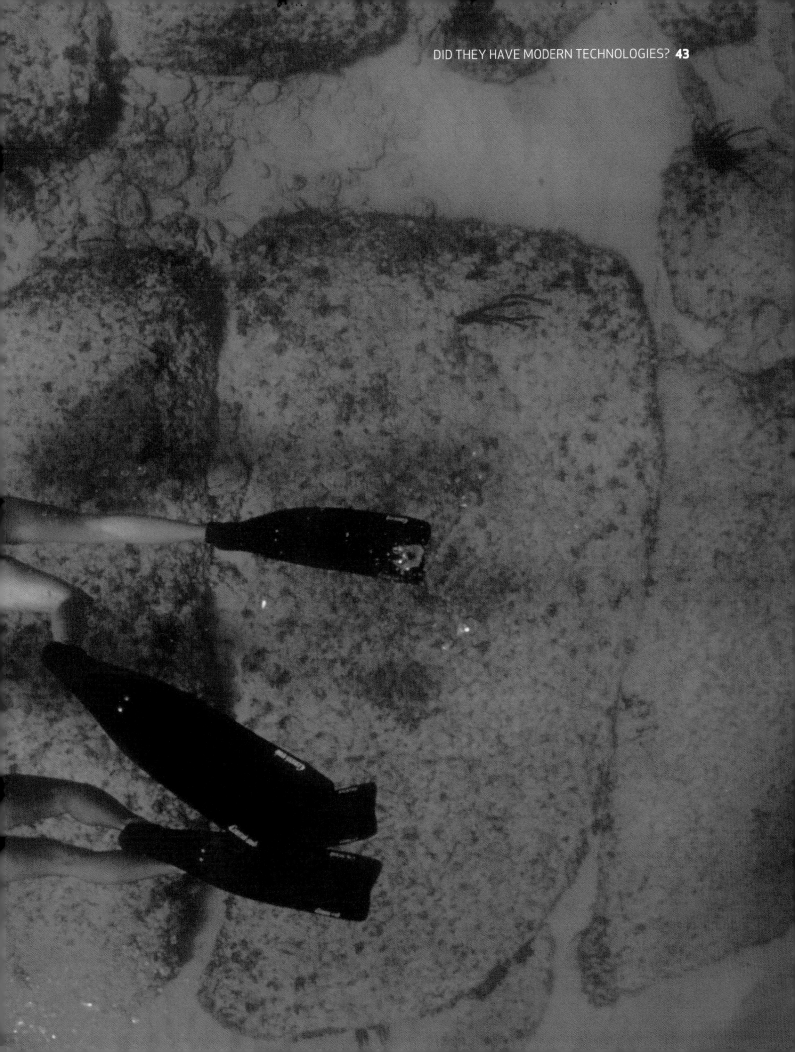

Alternative Hypotheses

Does the Church Accept the Existence of Atlantis?

During the Middle Ages, the Catholic Church emphatically dismissed the historical veracity of Atlantis, as well as of any human civilization that was not legitimized by Biblical texts. For one, in strictly chronological terms, the existence of a civilization almost five thousand years before the creation of the world as stated in Genesis, considered by the church to have occurred around 5500 BCE, could not be accepted without posing a serious theological contradiction. Subsequent scientific proof of human existence on Earth long before the Biblical record caused some religious people to venture into the study of lost civilizations, accepting the credibility of societies older than previously accepted. Toward the middle of the seventeenth century, the Jesuit Athanasius Kircher became a religious pioneer for the acceptance of the existence of Atlantis, and sketched a map of its territory in a portion of the Atlantic Ocean situated between Spain and the Caribbean islands, occupied by the Azores islands. Kircher indicated that the island had sunk, and made the map following texts from Plato and the Egyptians. A respected scholar, Athanasius Kirchner had the personality traits and skills to do something so audacious for his time. He was an extremely intelligent man, who spoke various languages and studied numerous disciplines including medicine, astronomy, philology, music, optics, and physics. He was also a professor of archaeology at the Roman College, and the inventor of the sundial.

ERUDITE
Athanasius Kircher was an archetype of the restless scholar. Among his passions was the study of the causes of volcanic eruptions.

Who Was the First Monarch of Atlantis?

According to an account handed down from Plato, the first king of the region and its waters was Atlas. When Poseidon decided to hand over power to a member of his vast lineage, he assigned the oldest to be king and gave him the Atlantic name. The god of water then assigned the far end of the island, opposite the Pillars of Hercules, to Atlas' brother Eumelus. The rest of the kings, of whom there were ten in total, were the descendants of these first ones: Amferes, Evaimon, Mineseas, Autoctono, Elasippus, Mestor, Azaes and Diaprepes. According to Plato's account, the king was always the most senior authority and his firstborn son took his place when he died. Together, they made up the divine Atlantis aristocracy, reigning over the ten internal regions of an empire which extended from what is now the Strait of Gibraltar to Egypt. A record of family conflicts does not exist, and everything points to the fact that in the Atlantis dynasty, peace ruled as well as the divine right to succession. According to myth, personal ambitions broke the harmony toward the end.

Was Atlantis a Group of Several Islands?

Accounts of Atlantis describe a floating island in the Atlantic, with an immense surface area almost the size of the Mediterranean sea. The descriptions are not unanimous, but the mention of a population of more than 50 million inhabitants suggests an immense territory. Additionally, the description of a ring structure proposes a design made up of circular islands, one inside another. The latter description is true to the narrative of Plato, and the mythological origin of Atlantean civilization, although some Atlantis scholars take it merely as a reference to a capital of sorts. The subject is controversial among the experts. If Atlantis had an immense territory leading to the name "the lost continent," geological records of its location should be more convincing, along with the discovery of underwater archaeological sites. The possibility of exaggeration regarding the dimensions of Atlantis is on the table.

Does Tiahuanaco Have a Connection to Atlantis?

Some researchers speculate about the possibility that the fantastic island could have existed on the South American continent or very close to its coast. In 1966, underwater cameras located large structures that had sunk to two thousand meters underwater off the coast of Peru. Other Atlantis experts have placed the possible construction of the Atlantic civilization in Tiahuanaco (Bolivia), basing their statement on the fact that they have discovered metal similar to orichalcum in the area, as per Plato's accounts. Other authors speculate that geological movements, which might have been the consequence of more extensive geological upheaval, could have destroyed Atlantis. We know that the city of Tiahuanaco exists on a

surface which, between ten and twelve thousand years ago – a date which coincides with the disappearance of Atlantis – was at an elevation of around 10,000 ft (3,048 m), lower than its current altitude. It is also believed that large geological movements changed the physiognomy of the Andes mountain range, elevating Lake Titicaca, and almost completely destroying the civilizations that could have been developed there. While at one point the earth's geography was raised, at another point the opposite took place.

PIONEER
Tiahuanaco is considered the original culture of all America.

Do Literary Accounts Prove Its Existence?

Prestigious authors such as William Shakespeare and Francis Bacon approach the subject of Atlantis in their literary works from different perspectives. The former alludes in *The Tempest* (1611) to the existence of lost islands in the ocean; the latter, in *The New Atlantis*, (1638), places the civilization as described by Plato on the American continent. Modern authors who wrote on the subject did so based on pre-existing conjectures, and did not add elements which could have resulted in scientifically plausible advances on the issue. The work that has contributed the most to popularizing the myth is *Twenty Thousand Leagues Under the Sea*, a book that the French author Jules Verne published in two parts in 1869 and 1870. Verne developed the fantasy story detailing the expedition of Captain Nemo, in command of a submarine christened Nautilus. The captivating story was adapted into a cinematic production early on, followed by a film by the French director Georges Méliès in 1907. The story returned to the big screen in 1916 (Stuart Paton) and in 1954 (Walt Disney).

Did Columbus know about Atlantis?

The real or fictitious existence of Atlantis was well-known in European expedition circles of the fifteenth century. The maps that guided the adventurers, travelers, and explorers noted the presence of various islands in the Caribbean which, according to the maps, had diverse names, though Antillas, Antilha, and Antiglia were the most common. According to what is known, Columbus was familiar with those maps, and as was noted by López de Gomara in his *General History of the Indies*, he was also familiar with Plato's texts Timaeus and Critias. All of this feeds the speculation that Columbus expected to discover, if not Atlantis itself, another island which may have inherited Atlantean culture. It is also plausible that the maritime empire of the Iberian peninsula held the same expectation, greedy as they were for markets and sources of exotic raw materials. From their perspective, the Indies or the legend of Atlantis spoke of paradises to be conquered.

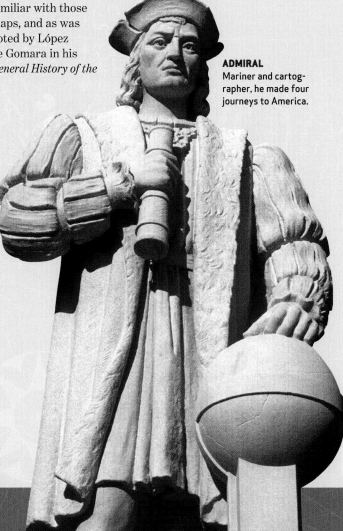

ADMIRAL
Mariner and cartographer, he made four journeys to America.

Was the Bimini Crystal the Work of the Atlanteans?

After discoveries in the depths near the Bahamas in 1968, scores of underwater explorers threw themselves into the exploration of these coasts. In 1970, Dr. Ray Brown, who had already explored Spanish galleons and treasures in the area, found something unheard of. After a storm, the navigation equipment and the compasses went "crazy." He saw some constructions under the water and he dove into the water with other divers. At a depth of less than 131 feet (211 m), a pyramidal shape sparkled like a mirror. Near its peak there was an entrance. A short tunnel led into an internal room. In the center, a crystal held by two metallic hands shone. The crystal sphere, subjected to hundreds of tests, did not reveal when or how it was made. It was revealed, however, that the energy that passed through it increased. Its first viewers described different sensations: they perceived breezes of different temperatures surrounding the crystal, as well as lights, voices and a prickly feeling on their skin.

COLLECTIVE UNCONSCIOUS
Jung stressed a language common to the entire human race, manifested in symbols.

Can Mediums Discover Atlantis?

The Swiss psychologist Carl Gustav Jung conceived the idea that all of the experiments and knowledge that constitute the common heritage of humanity occupy a place that he called the "collective unconscious." The concept allowed him to explain paraphysical experiences, which were in fashion in that period, such as the work of "mediums" who, in a state of trance, spoke unknown languages and referred to knowledge of lost civilizations. Between 1923 and 1944, the American psychic Edgar Cayce had a series of extrasensory experiences which he called "readings," during which he discovered a submerged continent located in the Bahamas, the peaks of the western region of Atlantis, which he called Poseidia. He left thousands of records of his telepathic communications behind, and 700 of them were of his vision of Atlantis. In Cayce's version, Atlantis was a society divided into two factions that were permanently at war,

ultimately causing the collapse of this civilization. His "reading" in 1932 established the geographical position of Atlantis in the following manner: " ... it can be found between the Gulf of Mexico and the Mediterranean. Evidence of this civilization can be found in the Pyrenees and Morocco, Honduras, Yucatán, and North America. In the Bahamas, it can be seen to this day."

To See and Visit

▼ **OTHER PLACES OF INTEREST**

THE GIBRALTAR MUSEUM
GIBRALTAR

It has been proposed that Atlantis consisted of a peninsula plus an archipelago which went from the Pillars of Hercules (Gibraltar) to the northwestern coasts of Africa. The rich past of Gibraltar can be seen reflected in its vast archaeological records, the study of which is directed and regulated by the museum. It has a wide range of archaeological research projects, among which is: The Pillars of Hercules and the Phoenicians.

BIMINI MUSEUM
ALICE TOWN, THE BAHAMAS

It has been believed that the island community making up North, South, and East Bimini once belonged to the road system of the lost city of Atlantis. The museum, located in the city of Alice Town on the North Island of Bimini and dedicated to the preservation of the history and culture of the people of the islands, is worth visiting. It has a valuable collection of utensils and other objects, some of which were discovered amongst nearby coral reefs, and which illustrate the history of the archipelago. Praised for its archives, documents, photos and varied artifacts, the museum is one of the biggest tourist attractions on the islands.

BRITISH MUSEUM
LONDON

It is one of the oldest and most famous museums of ancient artifacts in the world. There, more than seven million objects can be found,

Possible Locations

DOÑANA PARK

A team of researchers led by the U.S. archaeologist Richard Freund says that solid evidence has been found suggesting that Atlantis is located underneath the swamps of the Doñana National Park in Spain. According to them, the city would have been located to the north of Cádiz – in the Spanish Atlantic – around 55 miles (89 km) inland. A tsunami may have finished off the city. Notable among the evidence found were statuettes from the Bronze Age, and a series of measurements which indicate the existence of structures in the subsoil, which may have been canals.

BIMINI

The North Bimini and South Bimini islands make up the chain of the Bahamas, located approximately 50 miles (80 km) from Miami. Surrounded by a crystalline ocean, it attracts sailors and tourists, and particularly divers. In the 1960s, the accidental discovery of ancient structures submerged nearby were soon associated with Atlantis, and created a new reason to visit the islands.

SANTORINI

This is a volcanic Greek island in the Aegean Sea. Also known by the ancient name of Thera, it is a touristic paradise with white houses and Mediterranean architecture.

Yonaguni

In 1985, a diver discovered by chance an enormous stone construction submerged off the south coast of the island of Yonaguni, in the Japanese Ryukyu archipelago. A debate began at the time which has not yet reached a conclusion: Is this a natural structure, formed as a result of erosion? Or, is it a human creation which sank as the result of an earthquake? In the latter case, its purpose is unknown.

from every continent. Varied exhibits about ancient cultures from all over the world can be enjoyed, as well as other exhibits on sacred images and sacred works of art and collections of objects and utensils of unimaginable historic, cultural and artistic value. In the museum, a piece of the Great Sphinx of Giza can be found, which some have linked to the people of Atlantis.

NATIONAL ARCHAEOLOGICAL MUSEUM OF ATHENS
GREECE

It contains archaeological objects discovered in Greece from prehistory to late antiquity. It has the richest existing collection of objects from ancient Greece, from sculptures to urns and small objects. Inside the museum, you can visit the library, which has a valuable collection of records of archaeological excavations and is the most significant archive of publications on Greek archaeology.

THERA PREHISTORIC MUSEUM
SANTORINI, GREECE

It has a collection of frescos and objects discovered at the archaeological site of ancient Akrotiri, during the excavations done with the support of the Archaeological Society of Athens. It also has objects found during the first excavations in Potamos. Part of the collection – vases, cups and jugs – are delicately painted with familiar motifs, which can also be found on the murals of the city, from women dressed in Minoan dresses to scenes of the city.

An Enigma Beyond Legend

When I started investigating the Bermuda Triangle 21 years ago, I quickly discovered that the strongest barrier to accepting its existence and unraveling its mysteries was a very simple thing. We don't know what it is; this is to say, we replaced the actual mysteries of the Triangle with our own popular interpretations and theories. In essence, we created a legend. But the legend and the enigma of the Bermuda Triangle are not the same thing.

The Bermuda Triangle is really only two things. One, it is a geographic area of the North Atlantic Ocean off the southeast coast of the United States. It occupies the general area around the island of Bermuda, southern Florida and the island of Puerto Rico in the West Indies. Two, it is the enigma that this area of ocean is the place where most ships and planes completely vanish in fair weather for no readily explainable reason. The legend is fun, entertaining and sometimes educational. But the enigma of the Triangle is quite true, and it can be quite disturbing sometimes. This requires study and explanation. The many disappearances may often be used to support supernatural theories, but the Bermuda Triangle is not a paranormal subject. After 21 years, I've grown tired of being labeled a "paranormal researcher." I am most certainly not! The Bermuda Triangle is a mystery of this world. It is a tangible, hardcore mystery of hundreds of missing vessels and aircraft and thousands of lives lost. Perhaps that's why the Triangle is such a controversy at times. These ships and planes were real. They were thousands of tons of metal. Their disappearances are not suggestive reports as in UFOs or Bigfoot or other popular world mysteries. The Bermuda Triangle is, fact, the most tangible world mystery we have, for it is testified to by the total disappearance of hundreds of solid objects: they utterly vanished, some in circumstances that test our beliefs.

For instance, aircraft have vanished while coming in for a landing. In one case it happened with lightning-like suddenness. The tower controller had merely shifted his glance from the window to the radar screen. But when he looked back the plane was mysteriously gone. There are many others: aircraft have disappeared while ascending, yet radar captures no trace of them falling to earth; ships and planes have vanished over shallow water, and yet leave no trace in the clear waters only feets deep; one boat, the *Witchcraft*, vanished within 19 minutes of its radio distress to the Coast Guard and their arrival at the scene. The boat had built-in floatation and was unsinkable, but there was no trace ever found of it.

These are the genuine mysteries of the Triangle. It is not just the number that has attracted my attention, but the unusual nature of the disappearances. In many ways investigating these is like investigating an unsolved murder in a big city. The number of crimes is not as piquing as the nature of the scene of the crime. For the Bermuda Triangle disappearances, we are left with many puzzling clues. Often they don't add up to just common accident. But that does not mean they are supernatural. They are a stark reminder that we do not fully understand this globe that we live on. Mystery is not an invitation to spin tales of the supernatural and forsake learning. Mystery is an invitation to look and to learn. Mystery tells us there is something we do not yet know about this planet and this, of course, means there is something important we must discover.

 Many have lost their lives to inadvertently draw our attention to this planet's greater mysteries. If our study of these mysteries opens doors of knowledge to us, then they have not died in vain.

Gian J. Quasar

US Writer and essayist. Author of *Into the Bermuda Triangle: Pursuing the Truth Behind the World's Greatest Mystery* (2003). He has investigated more than 300 naval and aerial accidents occurring in the Bermuda Triangle and nearby areas over the last 20 years.

BERMUDA
Aerial view of coral reefs near the
Bermuda Islands, one of the vertices
of the celebrated Bermuda Triangle,
in which numerous ships and planes
have disappeared.

Disappearances in the Bermuda Triangle

Society's attraction to strange phenomena has not lessened in recent decades. The Bermuda Triangle is a milestone in this sense: few other occurrences have awakened such interest and filled so many pages.

Some 70% of the earth's surface is covered by water. A view of the terrestrial globe with the South Pole in the center shows a planet on which continents appear as small islands surrounded by an enormous blue mass, a color that almost monopolizes the earth's appearance from space. A distant extraterrestrial observer could easily deduce that the planet's surface is completely liquid. The oceans form an otherworld that still hides many mysteries for humanity. In the same way that extensive plateaus 16,000 feet (4,877 m) high and mountain ranges surpassing 26,000 feet (7,925 m) exist on dry land, an alternate world symmetrical to this one exists under the water; with plains 16,000 feet (4,877 m) deep and trenches reaching 36,000 feet (10,973 m), almost 8,000 feet (2,348 m) higher than

Everest, though in the opposite direction, and with icy conditions and no light, very little food, very low temperatures and pressure capable of crushing the strongest submarine. A hostile environment, one which shelters strange beings with terrifying features whose appearance has fed the imaginations of many generations of men fearful of the unknown.

In reality, of the 139 million square miles (360 million sq km) making up the Earth's liquid surface (130 times the size of Argentina), the human being barely understands the most superficial layer. What is known is owed to generations of sea explorers, from the intrepid inhabitants of the Marquesas Islands, who traveled 2,200 miles (3,541 km)in fragile rafts during the fourth century to colonize Easter Island, to the European explorers of the 15th and 16th centuries, who guided their sailing vessels to the coasts

of almost all exposed lands.

LIKE ANOTHER WORLD

Sub-surface exploration, however, is much more recent. Until well into the twentieth century, humankind's attitude toward what lay just over 30 ft below the water's surface varied between fear and indifference. As if it really were another world, humans have looked at the sea as those who see the mountain peaks surrounding them and choose to remain in the valley, ignorant but safe. Fortunately, in recent decades, scientific and technological advances enabled our lungs and eyes to be used in this hostile territory, which has opened the doors of a new world. With the help of sonar and modern bathyscaphes, the ocean floor has been mapped and creatures have been discovered; such as the sea spider, able to survive both the depth and the undersea environment, the frightening dragon fish, and the legendary

BAHAMIAN SHIPWRECK
High ship traffic in the waters of the Bermuda Triangle, combined with changeable weather, result in a large number of shipwrecks in the area.

giant clam, which really does exist and reaches up to 65 feet (19.8 m) across.

Knowledge of the undersea environment, in short, is still in its initial stages. Thus it is not strange that many areas of the planet's oceans have very high accident rates for our means of transport, and that due to the many hostile circumstances that can arise, diagnosis of incidents on the high seas can sometimes be very difficult.

A DANGEROUS COCKTAIL

One of these areas is called the Bermuda Triangle, which forms a polygon with three almost-equal sides having vertices in Miami, the largest city in Florida; San Juan, Puerto Rico, in the Antilles; and the Bermudas, a small archipelago located in the North Atlantic, more than 600 miles (966 km) from the coast of the United States. In this ocean region of more than a million 600,000 square miles (1,553,993 sq km), several factors interact: a sea floor with a diverse and unstable geography, high ship and plane traffic, a history rich in conflict and confrontation, and, most especially, a changing, dangerous climate.

Quite possibly, the most influential physical phenomenon in this area is the Gulf Stream, an enormous river 620 miles (998 km) wide and 325 feet (99 m) deep that captures the warm waters of the Gulf of Mexico and carries them to the coast of northern Europe, noticeably tempering the region's climate, which, by latitude, should be much colder, while also saving America's East Coast and the Antilles from becoming deserts, as well as determining the circulation of the dominant winds in the region.

The Gulf Stream runs north, along the eastern coast of the US and Canada, and delimits the western and northern borders of the Sargasso Sea, the only sea in the world with no coasts.

With a surface equivalent to two thirds of the United States and completely surrounded by a belt of ocean currents that move like clockwork, the Sargasso Sea, whose center is marked by the Bermuda Islands, has been the stuff of legends since the times of Christopher Columbus, as it occupies a vast region characterized by the prolonged calms that terrified sailors of an earlier era, a region that is a veritable cemetery for sail-powered ships. It is precisely these periods of total calm and the complete absence of wind that are responsible for the growth of massive seaweed forests on

LOST SHIP
Notice in a recreational port in the Bahamas, in March 1974, during the high point of interest in the mystery of the Bermuda Triangle.

HURRICANE BILL
An image of tropical cyclone Bill, in 2009, as it enters the waters of the triangle between Puerto Rico and the Bermudas.

the surface of the Sargasso Sea. These forests are populated by what the Portuguese call *sargaços* (sargasso), a seaweed that can get so dense as to make sailing difficult and even create the illusion that one has reached dry land. To the south of this sea, the danger is the opposite: The North Equatorial Current, returning to the Caribbean from the coasts of Africa, heats up as it moves west. The humidity from ocean winds, added to the warmth of the current, is the major cause of the hurricanes

that pound the coasts of the United States, the Caribbean, the Gulf of Mexico, and Central America annually, causing catastrophic damage as they pass.

This complex geographical context is one of the strongest arguments put forth by scientists to counter supernatural explanations for the numerous ship and plane accidents taking place in the Bermuda Triangle and nearby areas. The majority of these events, they posit, are related to climatic phenomena common to the region, such as

hurricanes, tropical storms and cyclones. Even so, many incidents have no scientific explanation. This is the case of the US brigantine *Mary Celeste*, which has become one of the biggest mysteries in the history of sailing and an example constantly cited by the most dedicated Triangle theorists, despite the fact that the ship sunk between the Azores Islands and Portugal, more than 3,000 miles (4,828 km) east of the Bermudas. One hundred feet in length, the *Mary Celeste* set sail from New York on November 5,

1872, loaded with 1,700 barrels of alcohol. One month later, it was found drifting by another ship, the *Dei Gratia*, with no one on board: neither the captain, his wife and daughter, nor the eight-member crew. The lifeboat was gone, but the cargo was intact: many personal objects were found, and there were provisions remaining for six months. The court judging the case put forth various hypotheses: a mutiny by the crew against the captain and his family, an act of piracy by the supposed discoverers of

Continued on page 60 ▶

The Geography of the Triangle

The ocean region delimited by the Bermuda Triangle and the terrain and water surrounding it has notably complex geography, with many topographical accidents, especially in an ocean that shifts from the dangerous Bahamian sand bars to a depth 28,000 feet (8,534 m).

The Bermuda Triangle

The area covered by the Bermuda Triangle is subject to a number of very powerful geographical and climatic factors that strongly influence flight and navigation in the area.

Sargasso Sea
This North Atlantic ocean region, which coincides with part of the Bermuda Triangle, is the only sea on the planet that has no coastlines, and is characterized by the dense layer of seaweed (called 'sargasso') that covers it and by the calm that slows the navigation of vessels crossing it.

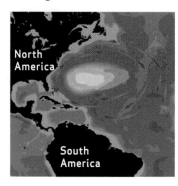

The Tongue of the Ocean
With hundreds of small islands, the Bahamas archipelago forms a shallow platform, penetrated by a large deep area called the 'Tongue of the Ocean' that separates the islands of Andros and New Providence, reaching a depth of 5,900 feet (1,798 m).

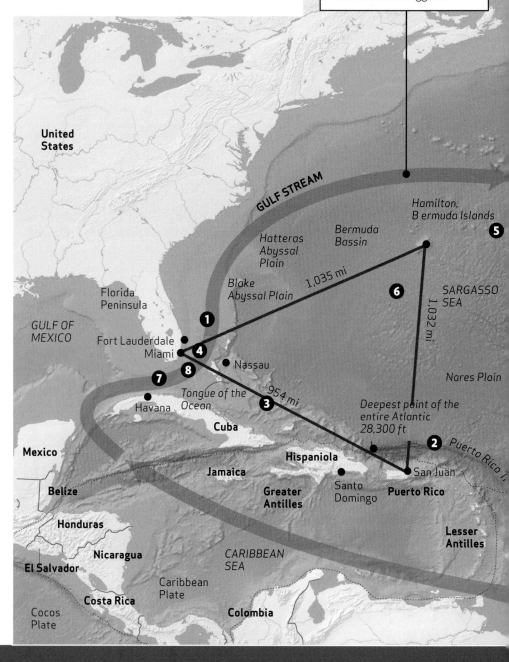

Gulf Stream
A huge mass of water crossing the North Atlantic from the Gulf of Mexico to Europe. It allows Europe to have a milder climate than its latitude would suggest.

United States

North America

South America

GULF STREAM

Hamilton, Bermuda Islands

5

Hatteras Abyssal Plain

Bermuda Bassin

SARGASSO SEA

Blake Abyssal Plain

1,035 mi

6

Florida Peninsula

GULF OF MEXICO

Fort Lauderdale
Miami

1

4

8

Nassau

1,032 mi

Nares Plain

7

Tongue of the Ocean

954 mi

3

Havana

Cuba

Deepest point of the entire Atlantic 28,300 ft

Mexico

Hispaniola

2

Puerto Rico I.

Jamaica

Santo Domingo

San Juan

Belize

Greater Antilles

Puerto Rico

Honduras

Lesser Antilles

Nicaragua

CARIBBEAN SEA

El Salvador

Caribbean Plate

Costa Rica

Cocos Plate

Colombia

Could Tsunamis Have Caused Some of the Disappearances in the Triangle?

The Puerto Rico Trench, located to the northeast of this island in the Antilles, is the deepest point of the fault between the North American and Caribbean tectonic plates. Movement in this very unstable area could cause a large tsunami that would strike the nearest coasts, such as the one that devastated Puerto Rico on October 11, 1918. However, there is no proof that a tsunami caused any of the disappearances in the Bermuda Triangle.

enigmas

Hurricanes
Atlantic tropical cyclones form off the west coast of Africa and gain energy as they move westward, activated by masses of humid air.

The path of hurricanes

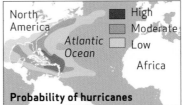

High
Moderate
Low

Probability of hurricanes

ATLANTIC OCEAN

Sohm Abyssal Plain

NORTH ATLANTIC CURRENT

The Azores

Mid-Atlantic Ridge

North American Plate

Eurasaian Plate

South American Plate

Cape Verde

Cape Verde Basin

CANARY CURRENT

NORTH EQUATORIAL CURRENT

Main disappearances
1. Flight 19
2. USS *Cyclops*
3. Carolyn Cascio's Cessna
4. The *Witchcraft*
5. The *Star Tiger*
6. The *Star Ariel*
7. SS *Marine Sulphur Queen*
8. The *Rubicon*

References
...... Tectonic Plates
⸺ The Bermuda Triangle

the abandoned ship, fear of the cargo exploding because of alcohol vapors from the hold... However, investigators could not determine for certain what happened.

Mysteries such as this one from 1872, and the many others like it that have occurred since, allowed a group of US researchers to string together a series of hypotheses in the mid-twentieth century that had almost nothing to do with possible meteorological or human causes. In 1964, the writer Vincent Gaddis (1913–1997) was the first to use the expression "Bermuda Triangle" to describe this area of the North Atlantic where so many ships and planes have sunk or disappeared with no apparent scientific cause. His article appeared in a pulp fiction magazine called *Argosy*, and began with a question that has received very diverse answers over the years: "What is it in this particular portion of the planet that has destroyed hundreds of ships and planes without leaving a trace?" Ten years later, in 1974, the writer Charles Berlitz released the book *The Bermuda Triangle*, which became a best seller. With several million copies sold, the mystery of the Triangle escaped from the small esoteric circles it had inhabited and reached the broader public. What reasons did Gaddis, Berlitz and later researchers put forth, each of them convinced that there was much more than hurricanes, pirates and cyclones in the area? One of the causes proposed is connected to one of humanity's greatest enigmas: the sinking of Atlantis. Citing specialist Edgar Cayce, Berlitz speculated that on the ocean floor, probably near the Bahamian coast, exists a powerful force (crystals, according to Cayce) that provided energy to the lost continent and now exercises a gravitational pull responsible for alterations in the function of compasses onboard ships and planes.

EXTRATERRESTRIAL ABDUCTIONS

Another of the causes most often repeated by specialists is the presence of extraterrestrials, who abduct entire ships, occasionally taking only their crews. Their activities are responsible for the elevated number of disappearances leaving behind no trace and the existence of ghost ships like the *Mary Celeste*. Something similar to an encounter of the third kind is what pilot Bruce Gernon experienced on board his aircraft in 1970. He was flying over the Bahamas when he saw some kind of tunnel inside a strange cloud. After exiting the phenomena, he realized that he had, in maybe just three minutes, covered a distance that would have taken a half hour under normal conditions. Gernon concluded that he had witnessed a space-time rift, and that, unlike most planes experiencing this, he had returned to tell about it: the others were now in another dimension, maybe the Super-Sargasso Sea, proposed by para-scientific investigator Charles Hoy Fort (1874–1932) as the destination of lost items.

Despite the disparities in these arguments, the high number of mysterious disappearances in the Bermuda Triangle has caught the attention of rigorous scientific organizations such as the US Coast Guard and the National Geographic Society, who cites the phenomena in their prestigious World Atlas. However, researchers from these organizations and many others refute the theories of Berlitz and company. Many believe that if an identical triangle is drawn in any other ocean in the world, the number of incidents and disappearances would be similar. In fact, the records of Lloyd's insurance company, traditionally specializing in sailing, record an incident rate in the Bermuda Triangle similar to that of any other

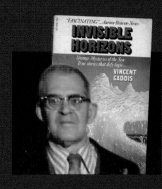

Vincent Gaddis
1913–1997

Author of the fortunate expression "Bermuda Triangle," Gaddis was a freelance writer who analyzed the subject in an article appearing in Argosy magazine in February of 1964. One year later, he released a book on the mysteries of the sea, titled *Invisible Horizons*, in which he covered the same topic.

INSPIRATION Gaddis copied Charles Fort (1874–1932), who wrote about esoteric topics and introduced the concept of the "Super-Sargasso Sea."

Steven Spielberg
1946

After *Duel* (1971) and *Jaws* (1975), this American filmmaker cemented his worth as a director with *Close Encounters of the Third Kind* (1977), a film featuring actors Richard Dreyfuss, François Truffaut, Melinda Dillon, and Teri Garr in which Spielberg explored human contact with extraterrestrial visitors. The director was inspired by the events of Flight 19 and the disappearance of the ship Cotopaxi – two of the strongest arguments for the Bermuda Triangle – when he wrote this sci-fi film.

POPULARIZATION Spielberg was inspired by some of the incidents from the Triangle in his film *Close Encounters of the Third* Kind.

◀ *Continued from page 57*

Continued on page 64 ▶

Charles Berlitz

A linguist and the grandson of the founder of the renowned language academies carrying his name, Charles Berlitz was born in New York in 1914 and died in Tamarac, Florida, in 2003, and is famous for his essays on paranormal topics. Despite the fact that he also wrote about Atlantis, the Roswell phenomena and the Philadelphia experiment (invisibility and teletransportation), the greatest success of his career was beyond doubt *The Bermuda Triangle* (1974), a book in which he analyzed a series of cases of ships and planes that vanished in this area, dissecting the official reports made by the Coast Guard and suggesting alternative causes related to extraterrestrials, strange magnetic forces, and the remains of ancient civilizations. Despite the fact that the book sold millions of copies globally and was key in popularizing the subject, other authors criticized it severely for the lack of authenticity surrounding Berlitz's theories and much of the information presented.

DIFUSSION Charles Berlitz graduated cum laude from Yale University and supposedly spoke 32 languages. His greatest contribution was the popularization of the enigma of the Bermudas through his book *The Bermuda Triangle*, published in 1974.

1914–2003

"In no other area have there been so many unexplainable disappearances as in the Bermuda Triangle."
Charles Berlitz

Edgar Cayce
1877–1945

Berlitz and other authors cite Edgar Cayce, an American clairvoyant, when analyzing one of the possible causes of the disappearances in the Bermuda Triangle. Well-known in the United States in the first half of the twentieth century for his predictions about the future, Cayce answered questions about esoteric topics while in a hypnotic trance, an ability supposedly acquired while in a coma caused by being struck by a ball at five years old. In 1940, Cayce predicted that Atlantis would reemerge from its sub-aquatic exile in 1968 near the Bahamas. That very year, something resembling a pyramid was discovered near Andros Island, leading specialists in the subject to recall his prediction and use his "expertise" to revindicate the relationship between the lost continent and the disappearance of ships and planes in the Bermuda Triangle.

ENDURING PROPHET In conferences on Atlantis, Cayce spoke of crystals that provided energy to the lost continent and were still active under the water's surface.

Major Disappearances

Since the time investigations of the high number of accidents on and over the waters of the Bermuda Triangle began, there have been thousands of incidents. The 1945 disappearance of Flight 19, a squadron of Grumman TBM Avenger aircraft, is the most famous.

The disappearance of Flight 19

The Grumman TBM Avenger was a torpedo plane used by the US Air Force and Navy from 1942. A pilot, a gunner and a radio operator made up the crew. Flight 19 was led by Lieutenant Charles Taylor.

THE SQUADRON'S FINAL FLIGHT

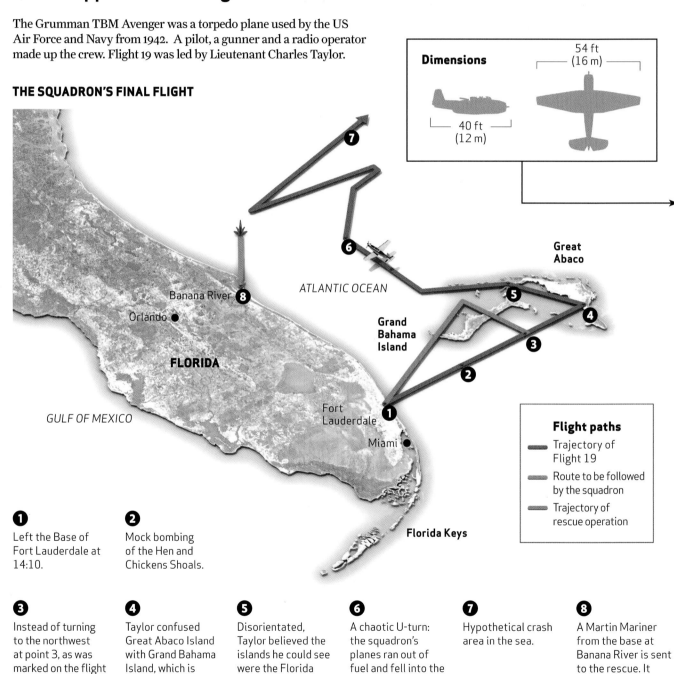

Dimensions

54 ft (16 m)

40 ft (12 m)

Great Abaco

ATLANTIC OCEAN

Banana River ❽

Orlando ●

Grand Bahama Island

❺

❹

❻

❸

FLORIDA

❷

GULF OF MEXICO

Fort Lauderdale ❶

Miami ●

Florida Keys

Flight paths

— Trajectory of Flight 19

— Route to be followed by the squadron

— Trajectory of rescue operation

❶ Left the Base of Fort Lauderdale at 14:10.

❷ Mock bombing of the Hen and Chickens Shoals.

❸ Instead of turning to the northwest at point 3, as was marked on the flight plan, the squadron continued straight ahead.

❹ Taylor confused Great Abaco Island with Grand Bahama Island, which is where he should have been going.

❺ Disorientated, Taylor believed the islands he could see were the Florida Keys, south of the peninsula.

❻ A chaotic U-turn: the squadron's planes ran out of fuel and fell into the sea.

❼ Hypothetical crash area in the sea.

❽ A Martin Mariner from the base at Banana River is sent to the rescue. It explodes in the air within minutes.

What Caused Lieutenant Taylor's Disorientation at the Head of Flight 19?

The Avengers in Flight 19 already had gyroscopes oriented towards the geographical North Pole, not to the magnetic North Pole, as traditional compasses are. Also, all planes from that period had two or even three instruments for orientation using different mechanisms, so that if one failed, the pilot could rely on the others. Thus, Lieutenant Taylor's disorientation can only be attributed to nervousness or an exterior influence that knocked out all of the plane's indicators.

enigmas

CABIN OF THE AVENGER

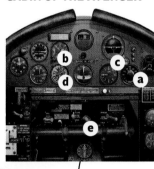

a **Radio-altimeter**
Shows the altitude of the aircraft above the ground.

b **Altimeter**
Marks the altitude above sea level.

c **Inclinometer**
Measures the inclination of the wings in relation to the earth's surface.

d **Anemometer**
Measures the speed of the aircraft relative to the air moving around it.

e **Directional Gyro**
Shows the direction that the plane is heading. It did not work on Flight 19.

Grumman TBM Avenger
It was tough, stable, easy to maneuver, had an excellent radio and remarkable endurance.

Technical Specifications

Empty Weight	10,694 lbs (4,850 kg)
Crew	3 people
Fuel tank	335 gal (1,268 liters)
Range (empty)	1,214 mi (1,953 km)
Maximum speed	270 mph (434 kmh)
Maximum altitude	23,400 ft (7,132 m)

OTHER NOTABLE DISAPPEARANCES

***Star Tiger* (Jan, 1948) and *Star Ariel* (Jan, 1949)**
The *Star Tiger* airliner disappeared without a trace. A year later the same thing happened to *Star Ariel*.

SS *Marine Sulphur Queen* (Feb, 1963)
This merchant ship disappeared in the Florida Keys, with a crew of 39 people and a load of molten sulphur.

USS *Cyclops* (Mar, 1918)
One of the world's largest freighters sank with 308 people and a cargo of manganese. The Navy called it "disconcerting."

The Cessna 172 of Carolyn Cascio (Jun, 1964)
Cascio's last words: "This should be Grand Turk, but there's nothing down there, no airport, no houses... nothing."

Corsair Territory

Since the beginning of European colonization of the American continent, piracy has been, alongside meteorological phenomenon, the major cause of incidents on the high seas in the Atlantic. In the sixteenth and seventeenth centuries, corsairs (pirates with a license to plunder) were no more than mercenaries from enemy nations, usually Britain, France or Holland, that attacked Spanish and Portuguese ships laden with gold and other riches from the Americas. Over time, many of them took up residence in the Antilles and the Caribbean. The island of Tortuga, north of Haiti, became a legendary pirate bastion from which the corsairs departed on pillaging expeditions that left numerous ships empty of cargo and crew, floating at the mercy of the currents. Many legends from the area, disconcerting precursors to the Bermuda Triangle, sprang from these pirate raids.

THE GULF STREAM
Eighteenth-century map showing the current's path across the Atlantic.

ATLANTIC STORM
Engraving from the nineteenth century evoking Columbus's voyage across the sea.

Who Discovered the Sargasso Sea?

There is no irrefutable documentation of any European captain crossing the Sargasso Sea before Christopher Columbus. The Vikings had crossed the Atlantic previously, but at latitudes much further north. Columbus and his crew were, then, the first Europeans to experience the calms so characteristic of the Sargasso Sea and the abundance of seaweed so thick it sometimes looked as though they had reached dry land. On Columbus's third voyage to America, in 1498, he enlisted an Andalusian named Antón de Alaminos as cabin boy for the expedition. Years later, under Hernán Cortés, Antón became the first pilot in history to use the Gulf Stream to return to Europe.

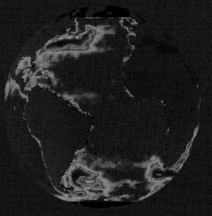

TRIPS FROM AMERICA TO EUROPE
At the time of sailing, the boats took advantage of the Gulf Stream and prevailing northwest winds to go to Europe.

area. And, of course, Lloyd's charges no high-risk premium for frequenting this sector.

Despite this, many of the causes official investigators have attributed to these accidents may seem to some equally as convoluted as those given by defenders of the supernatural. In addition to reasons such as climatic phenomena,

◀ Continued from page 60

piracy, cyclones, human navigational error, acts of war or the residual effects of conflicts (abandoned mines or bombs that explode), illnesses or the explosion of dangerous cargo, one finds more unusual reasons such as: ergot poisoning or St. Anthony's fire caused by a fungus growing on rye bread, the aptly named clear-air turbulences, the whirl winds generated in the numerous blue holes of the Bahamas, or the methane gas bubbles released from the ocean sub-floor that proved capable of sinking a BP oil rig in the Gulf of Mexico.

The truth is that, due to widespread use of technologies such as sonar and GPS in aviation and sailing, the number of accidents with no explanation has declined noticeably, but there are always a certain number of incidents whose investigations are closed without reaching a conclusion and become a part of the mysteries of the great unknown we call the sea.

GERARD CROISET
The well-known Dutch para-psychologist, right, during a conference on the Bermuda Triangle. In his heyday, Croiset was in high demand, an expert on finding missing persons.

A High-Risk Area

Off the coasts of Florida alone, the US Coast Guard receives an average of 700 calls for assistance every month. To this, add a considerable number of combat aircraft that have fallen during maneuvers, such as those of Flight 19.

The TBM's Floating Ability

One of the largest controversies regarding the infamous Flight 19 was the ability of the TBM Avenger to float. While some authors, including Berlitz, rely on images such as those shown below to demonstrate that the plane could float long enough to deploy the lifeboats it carried, others insist that the machine would have sunk in a matter of seconds.

SHIPWRECKS The ever greater numbers of explorers reaching the ocean floor are surprised by the large number of ships and planes resting on the bed of the continental platform.

What Happened to Flight 19?

The case of Flight 19, from the Fort Lauderdale station in Florida, is undoubtedly the most often cited and mysterious of the broad range of incidents legitimizing the mystery of the Bermuda Triangle.

On December 5, 1945, four months after the end of World War II, a squadron of five Grumman TBM Avenger torpedo bombers took off from the US Naval base in Fort Lauderdale, north of Miami, for a routine two-hour training flight during which the planes would travel some 300 miles (483 km) before returning to base.

Some 20 minutes after taking off, heading east, the squadron performed the pre-defined bombing maneuvers over some islets, after which the planes were to veer north, and then west, to complete the mission. However, at 3:45 pm, the time at which, according to the flight plan, the bombers were to be returning to base, the base received the first worrisome message from the squadron commander, Lieutenant Charles Taylor: "Emergency. We seem to be off course. Cannot see land." In response to the control tower's suggestion to veer west, the Lieutenant responded: "We don't know which direction is west. Everything is wrong. Everything is strange. Even the ocean looks strange." Shortly after 4:20 pm, having heard nothing more from the planes in Flight 19, the command center realized that the planes had only four more hours of flight time before running out of fuel and plummeting into the sea. A massive rescue operation involving hundreds of ships and planes was immediately initiated. These vessels spent the next three days combing more than 200,000 square miles (500,000 square kilo-meters), an area three times the size of Uruguay, in the Atlantic Ocean and the Gulf of Mexico. The result? Not a trace of the five Avengers, whose fatal destiny also claimed one of the rescue planes taking off that day, a Martin Mariner hydroplane that exploded shortly after takeoff.

In a US society very conscious of the armed forces after WWII, the commotion over this disappearance was tremendous. Despite the fact that no one talked explicitly about the Bermuda Triangle at that time, this being 19 years before Vincent Gaddis coined the term in his article in *Argosy* magazine, the doctor Joseph Manson Valentine, an expert in paranormal phenomena, alerted the Miami News that the crew of Flight 19 "are still there, but in a different dimension, caught

enigmas

Do the remains found in 1991 belong to Flight 19?

In 1991, the discovery of the remains of several Avenger planes some 12 miles (19 km) off the coast of Florida in approximately 750 ft (229 m) of water by the submersible Deep Sea, designed by British engineer Graham Hawkes, put Flight 19 on the front page of local and national news once again. However, the serial numbers of the planes, which were difficult to find due to the remains' advanced state of decomposition, did not match those of Flight 19, but belonged to a squadron lost two years earlier, on October 9, 1943, during World War II. The mystery of Flight 19 continues to lay somewhere off the coast of Florida.

FAILED RESCUE
Dick Adams, a retired Army pilot, examines a map on which the Bermuda Triangle is marked while relating his experiences during the rescue attempt for the five Avengers of Flight 19.

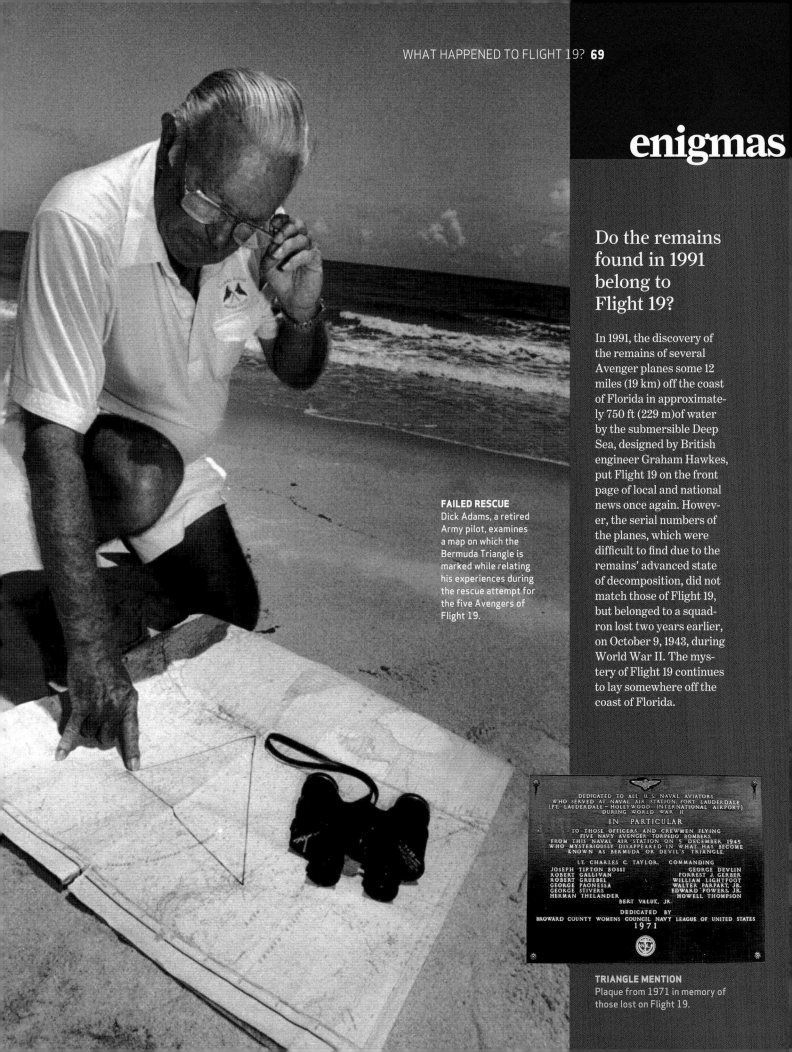

DEDICATED TO ALL U.S. NAVAL AVIATORS
WHO SERVED AT NAVAL AIR STATION, FORT LAUDERDALE
(FT. LAUDERDALE — HOLLYWOOD INTERNATIONAL AIRPORT)
DURING WORLD WAR II

IN PARTICULAR

TO THOSE OFFICERS AND CREWMEN FLYING
FIVE NAVY AVENGER TORPEDO BOMBERS
FROM THIS NAVAL AIR STATION ON 5 DECEMBER 1945
WHO MYSTERIOUSLY DISAPPEARED IN WHAT HAS BECOME
KNOWN AS BERMUDA OR DEVIL'S TRIANGLE

LT. CHARLES C. TAYLOR, COMMANDING

JOSEPH TIPTON BOSSI	GEORGE DEVLIN
ROBERT GALLIVAN	FORREST J. GERBER
ROBERT GRUEBEL	WILLIAM LIGHTFOOT
GEORGE PAONESSA	WALTER PARPART, JR.
GEORGE STIVERS	EDWARD POWERS, JR.
HERMAN THELANDER	HOWELL THOMPSON

BERT VALUK, JR.

DEDICATED BY
BROWARD COUNTY WOMENS COUNCIL NAVY LEAGUE OF UNITED STATES
1971

TRIANGLE MENTION
Plaque from 1971 in memory of those lost on Flight 19.

Who Spoke with Taylor?

Even today, more than 50 years after the incident, there is a great deal of confusion over the number of people who were in contact with Flight 19 commander Lieutenant Charles Taylor by radio. In addition to the previously indicated communications with the Fort Lauderdale air base controller, Charles Berlitz reproduces in his best seller, *The Bermuda Triangle*, the 1974 revelations of journalist and writer Arti Ford, according to which Taylor had said, "Don't come for me... they seem to be from outer space...." No official investigation contains this phrase, and few Flight 19 researchers defend its accuracy. The communication that exists beyond a shadow of a doubt is that between Taylor and Lieutenant Cox, who was flying a plane in the area that day and heard Taylor's requests for help. Taylor explained to him that he believed himself to be over the Florida Keys, located around 300 miles south of his actual position. Cox turned south to get a visual of the squadron and guide them to the coast, but did not see any signs of them. Taylor also communicated with the Coast Guard base in Port Everglades, to the south of the air base. The controller there suggested allowing another plane from the squadron with a functional gyroscope to guide them, and urged Taylor to switch to the emergency frequency, as the conventional signal was beginning to fail due to the distance. Taylor, very confused at this point, neither responded nor put these suggestions into action, and continued his erratic trajectory over the Atlantic.

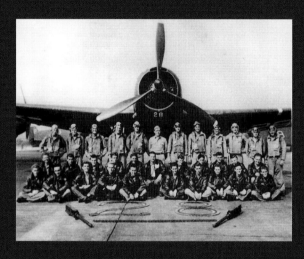

LOST
The members of the squadron lost on Flight 19 pose under one of the Grumman TBM Avengers.

"Unknown Causes"

The authorities of the US Navy investigating the case concluded that the disappearance of the five Avengers was due to operation commander Lieutenant Charles Taylor's disorientation. However, a few months later, the outrage of the family members of some of those lost caused the Naval attorney general to reopen the case and admit that Taylor had been declared guilty without conclusive proof. The incident was eventually attributed to unknown causes.

FAMILY
Susan Spengler and Joan Conlon, daughter and wife of Edward Powers, one of the 14 missing from Flight 19.

in a magnetic phenomenon that could have been caused by a UFO."
Investigators initiated inquiries to find a scientific reason for the incident, despite the fact that one of the officials in the Naval investigative committee admitted that the five Avengers "disappeared completely, as if they had flown to Mars. We have no idea what devilry is taking place there." Another of the committee members admitted to the

Frustrated Rescue

After losing contact with Flight 19, authorities at the Fort Lauderdale base ordered the departure of a Martin Mariner rescue hydroplane, capable of landing in very adverse weather conditions. With a crew of 13, the hydroplane sent several routine messages as it approached the area where it was believed that the five Avengers had fallen. After a few minutes, however, the tower stopped receiving communications from the Martin Mariner. The rescue plane seemed to have had the same luck as the squadron from Flight 19. It sent no message requesting help. Later, a ship stated that it had observed an explosion in the air at approximately the time the hydroplane ceased communicating with the base. In aeronautical circles, Martin Mariners were called "flying gas tanks."

MARTIN MARINER
An amphibious aircraft, identical to the one that disappeared in the Atlantic, remains afloat shortly after taking off from Virginia in 1943.

press later that "we couldn't even make a good guess as to what happened." Yes, they agreed that there had been a concatenation of errors and adverse circumstances: the failure of Taylor's compasses, failures in radio communications, the suddenly bad weather, nightfall...

A preliminary report blamed Lieutenant Taylor, especially after learning that just before the maneuvers began, the operations commander had asked to be relieved, without giving a reason for the request to his superiors. More than a half-century later, an investigation headed by British aerial accident specialist Phil Gilles concluded, after listening attentively to the recordings from that day, that Taylor was not in the appropriate mental state to lead the maneuvers, especially given that the rest of the squadron pilots were new pilots.

It is possible that the strong reigning tail wind pushed the squadron off of their initial course, and that, when they should have veered northwest to begin their return, the elongated shape of Great Abaco, similar to Grand Bahama and even the Florida Keys, confused Taylor, who was slowly losing the calm he needed to recover control of the situation.

Why Have So Many Ships Disappeared?

While the area in which they occur is of great importance in the disappearance of planes, weather is the decisive factor in the disappearance of ships, along with other more unusual causes.

Despite the fact that safety on the oceans has improved exponentially since the times when sail-powered ships reigned, in the 21st century there continue to be many shipwrecks, from small craft to yachts, fishing vessels, and even large ships weighing tons.

What is surprising is that in a large number of these accidents, both in the past and the present, the vessel disappears without a trace or becomes a derelict or ghost ship drifting along, with no clues as to what may have happened to the crew.

Such is the case of the *Mary Celeste* (1872), the most famous documented incident in the Bermuda Triangle, and the *Rosalie* (1840), the *Carrol A. Deering* (1921), the *Rubicon* (1944), the *City Belle* (1946), and the yacht *Connemara IV* (1955), all found with no passengers, but in perfect condition.

These circumstances have driven many researchers to consider the possibility that UFOs abducted the crew to study the intellectual and technological development of humans, as asserted by John W. Spencer in his 1969 best-seller *Limbo of the Lost*, and Scotsman Ivan T. Sanderson, known for his studies of the Loch Ness Monster.

In other documented cases, both the crew and the boat disappeared, or even the abduction of entire ships, facts that inspire the hypotheses of the most fervent devotees of the Bermuda Triangle.

One of the most mysterious events is that of the *Ellen Austin* (1881), an English ship that found an abandoned schooner in good condition in the middle of the Atlantic.

The captain put part of his crew onboard the ghost ship, and both vessels continued onward, traveling side by side. The ships were separated by fog for several days, and when the fog lifted, the ghost ship was again crewless.

MARINE CYCLONES
Ocean storms can be accompanied by dangerous cyclones.

GHOST SHIP
Ever since the legend of the Flying Dutchman, crafted in the seventeenth century, many abandoned ships have become interesting enigmas for researchers. Some of the most well-known cases were found in the waters of the Bermuda Triangle.

The Cyclops

"One of the Sea's Most Baffling Mysteries." This is how the disappearance of the cargo ship the USS *Cyclops*, one of the largest vessels in the world at the time, was described. The *Cyclops* sank in 1918 somewhere between Barbados and Virginia with 308 people on board and a cargo of manganese, a highly corrosive substance. It still has not been located. At the time, during WWI, there was talk of an assault by a German submarine, a mine explosion, mutiny, an attack by a giant octopus... Logic, on the other hand, points to an accident with the dangerous cargo, or capsizing during a storm, highly likely due to the ship's structure.

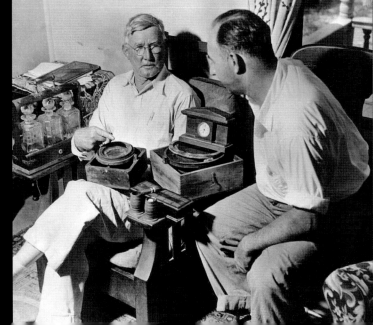

SHIP REMAINS
A retired sailor displays objects from vessels shipwrecked off the coast of Cape Hatteras (United States).

Guidance Instruments

From the very beginning, the history of navigation has been linked to developments in guidance instruments. Ancient navigators used simple observation of the sun, moon, and stars, and from then to the latter part of the twentieth century there was a progression to the use of GPS, a system that guarantees precision almost to the millimeter.

Safer

Triangle investigators are accustomed to looking back to the nineteenth century at instances of ships disappearing without logical explanation, although they often go back to the Age of Discovery or even to ancient times to find answers for the 'black legends' that surround certain maritime areas. However, shipwrecks from the beginnings of the nineteenth and twentieth centuries cannot be analyzed in the same way, since today's knowledge of the sea is much greater than that of navigators from the era of the first steamboats. The technology used by ships today allows a much greater range of control over the ships themselves, and over the hazardous environment found on the high seas, making navigation by boat much safer and the occurrence of disappearances without a clear cause much less frequent.

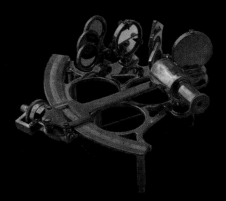

SEXTANT
This appeared in the eighteenth century to replace the astrolabe and measure angles between the sun, the North Star and the horizon. If you knew the time, you could determine latitude with some precision.

OLD COMPASS
The traditional compass indicates magnetic north with a magnetic needle. The fact that it did not indicate the geographic pole, located several degrees to the east, induced errors.

NAUTICAL CHART
Portolans, the medieval charts used to recognize coastlines became charts in the fifteenth century, when sailors set out across the open sea. This chart from the late sixteenth century shows the Triangle area, the Caribbean and the Gulf of Mexico.

MODERN COMPASS
Incorporating electronic technology has made it possible to correct the traditional error between magnetic and geographic north and increase the accuracy of measurements.

RADAR
Even though it is not exactly a navigation instrument, radar (acronym for radio detection and ranging) caused quite a revolution in navigation after it was first used toward the middle of the twentieth century. It is an electronic system that emits electromagnetic waves to measure distances, directions, and the speed of objects, both moving and stationary, such as boats and airplanes. This function has made it indispensable for air traffic control and meteorology.

Foucault's gyroscope

Invented in 1852 by French physicist Jean-Bernard Léon Foucault – who also invented the pendulum – for a demonstration of the earth's rotation, the gyroscope was not originally created as an orientation instrument. Foucault realized that it could well serve to indicate north if the movements of the base were fixed, since the apparatus would align itself with the meridian. The movements of this device served as a basis for reducing the rolling movements of ships.

QUADRANT
This was used from the fifteenth century to find the latitude by measuring the distance between the horizon and the sun or the North Star, but needed two people to operate it.

ASTROLABE
Created by Greek astronomers in the second century BCE, the astrolabe, a circle that lets you locate the stars and measure latitude from the time or vice versa, was widely used until the invention of the sextant.

CROSS-STAFF OR JACOB'S STAFF
Developed in the fourteenth century to make astronomical measurements, the cross-staff was a strip of wood that slid on a transverse stick. To measure the latitude, you had to point the device at the sun or the Pole Star and then move the transverse bar to coincide with the horizon.

GPS
Available commercially from the 1990s, it has meant a jump in navigation as decisive as the compass or sextant in their time. The system uses a complex structure of satellites to give the position with an error of less than 10 ft (3 m).

What Is the Origin of the Bimini Road?

Found near the island of North Bimini at a depth of 18 feet (5.5 meters)—is this road a work of nature? This mystery could all at once resolve two of the greatest mysteries of humanity: those of Atlantis and the Bermuda Triangle.

In 1968, Joseph Manson Valentine (1902–1994), zoologist, amateur archaeologist and specialist in paranormal occurrences, found a unique underwater rock formation while scuba diving just off west of North Bimini island, in the Bahamas. It seemed like a type of road, approximately 2,600 feet (792 m) long, made of rectangular limestone rocks. This formation, found 18 feet (5 m) deep and seemingly created by man, is not the only one of its kind. There are two other paths – both of which are cruder and narrower but do not run consistently as they have frequent gaps – situated between the main road and the beach, although as yet no connection between the three has been found. The first path was quickly designated as the Bimini Road or Bimini Wall. The stones forming this path are tabular blocks, 7 to 13 feet (2 to 4 m) in width, and fit together in a similar way to the walls constructed by the Incas at Cuzco and Macchu Picchu. News of the discovery spread like wildfire among the large esoteric community in the United States in that era. They did not hesitate to relate the find to the prophecy of psychologist and clairvoyant Edgar Cayce (1877–1945) – who had predicted that the ruins of Atlantis would be revealed in 1968 – and with the wave of boat and airplane disappearances in the Bermuda Triangle, which had become quite a popular subject after the publication of Vincent Gaddis' first article four years earlier.

Over the following months, a profusion of geologists, archaeologists, anthropologists and engineers made diving excursions into the waters surrounding Bimini to analyze the find. Investigations showed no evidence of tools being used to carve out the blocks. The bedrock surrounding the supposed paving was also examined. No traces were found of the canals or excavations that would normally be used to complete the road by pre-Colombian civilizations. Valentine and many other investigators refuted these conclusions, arguing that erosion from the water and sand could have erased any vestige of human tools, although geologists contest that this type of seemingly artificial rocky formation exists in other locations around the globe and is known as tessellated pavement.

The Mystery of the Andros Pyramid

In 1970, barely two years after the Bimini discovery, American diver Ray Brown claimed to have found a concavity in the shape of a pyramid under the waters of the island of Andros (inset photo), also in the Bahamas. In a central location of this pyramidal cave, Brown assured that he found a quartz sphere, which he brought to the surface and which supposedly had paranormal powers, a circumstance later confirmed by a few close friends of the diver. The enormous magnetic power of this crystal shown to interested members of the press, according to Brown, was the cause of the malfunctioning of compasses in the Bermuda Triangle and confirmed that Atlantis was located in the Bahamas. Apparently, Brown gave the crystal to his mentor shortly before he died, and today its location is unknown.

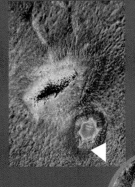

THE BIMINI ROAD
Two scuba divers swim over a section of the road, supposedly mysteriously constructed by human hands, found to the west of this island in the Bahamas.

Are There Aliens in the Triangle?

Due to official silence and government censure of independent investigations, many specialists maintain that the disappearances of boats and airplanes in the Triangle are due to extraterrestrial activity on the earth.

In 1966, the leaders of the US Air Force issued circular AFR 80-17 to all pilots, which was a series of instructions for conduct in the event of an encounter with a UFO. Officially, military and governmental leaders deny the existence of extraterrestrials operating on our planet, but among the inner circles they do admit that this is a possibility.

Many Triangle specialists link the presence of alien ships with the disappearance of ships and planes in the area. According to Berlitz, there have been reliable testimonies reporting UFO sightings in places and times that can be easily linked to incidents in the Triangle. John Spencer, a pilot for ten years in the Air Force, also supports this theory, arguing that the elevated traffic existing in the area allows the extraterrestrials to affect a significant number of ships and airplanes, far away from the large numbers of humans that live on land. Some of these authors assume the possibility that USOs (Unidentified Submersible Objects) also exist, and that these could have a base in the depths pf the ocean.

But, according to these investigators, what interest do aliens have in us? Spencer himself maintains that aliens allow human civilization to continue, although occasionally they abduct humans, airplanes and boats for the purpose of monitoring biological and technological evolution, with special attention to advancements in aeronautics.

Investigators say, however, that alien control over humankind long precedes our control of airspace, and they use as an example the various pieces of airships that are exhibited in the Museo de Oro in Bogotá and that belong to the Tairona culture, whose greatest period of achievement was around the year 1000 CE! Another investigator of the sightings of extraterrestrial ships, astronomer Morris K. Jessup, confirms that the disappearances of large ships such as the *Mary Celeste* or the *Ellen Austin* were caused by UFOs, and he describes the case of the Seabird, a giant sailboat that disappeared in the sea in 1850, ran aground on a beach as if it had been placed there by the hands of a giant, and then vanished again one night. After his investigation, Jessup concludes that all these changes in position could only be maneuvered from above.

enigmas

Abductions or Space-Time Jumps?

Aside from the disappearances without an obvious cause, the Triangle is ripe with other inexplicable phenomena, such as the space-time disruptions that numerous airplanes have experienced in the region. The case of Bruce Gernon, as related in the introduction, or that of a National Airlines Boeing 727, which disappeared off the radar screen of Miami airport for ten minutes then reappeared and landed without problems. The crew and the passengers did not notice anything, although all the clocks on the airplane were ten minutes behind. Morris Jessup believes that these disruptions are due to alien intervention. According to his hypothesis, the UFOs created a magnetic-time storm capable of disintegrating any object, in accord with what Einstein proposed in his unified field theory.

UFOS IN THE TRIANGLE
Extraterrestrial ships could cause space-time disruptions to abduct human ships.

An Antidote to the Mystery

Since its use began in the 1990s in both ships and airplanes, the Global Positioning System (GPS) has exponentially improved the orientation and navigation of the vessels that cross the ocean and has facilitated their location in the event of an emergency.

GPS

GPS (Global Positioning System) is a method of navigation by satellite by which the position of a person, object or means of transportation can be determined with great precision, at virtually any place on the planet, and with a very small margin of error, usually only a few feet. As is only logical, since the onset of the use of this technology – and others similar to it, such as the Russian Glonass or the European Galileo – the number of disappearances in the Bermuda Triangle and other trouble spots of the oceans has considerably diminished, since it has become more difficult to get lost, and locating the signal of a ship by third parties or by the communication center has become much easier.

1 TRIANGULATION
To determine the position of an object, GPS employs triangulation: determining the distance between the object and three satellites, and using these three numbers to easily calculate the coordinates.

2 DISTANCES
The GPS receiver captures the exact position issued by a satellite, which establishes distance by calculating the time the signals take to reach the receiver.

24 SATELLITES
The GPS system uses 24 satellites that cover the entire earth at an altitude of 87,205 feet (26,580 meters).

MEASUREMENT
All positions (latitude, longitude, and time) are calculated thanks to the signal of a minimum of four of the 24 available satellites.

COMMUNICATIONS CENTER
Equipped with powerful satellite dishes, this is the base for the systems on earth.

Highly diverse receivers

The GPS terminals or receivers indicate the user's current position. There are receivers for cars, boats, airplanes, even for people walking, and they are incorporated into many makes of mobile phones.

Digital cartography

Establishing the GPS global navigation system would have been impossible without the development of digital cartography, which is incorporated as software in all terminals that are marketed commercially. The image on the left shows the screen from the Russian icebreaker Kapitan Khlebnikov, in which a fragment of the coast of Antarctica is identifiable.

3 SYNCHRONIZATION
All the satellite systems are perfectly synchronized with each other and with the communications center by means of atomic clocks.

4 POSITION
The receiver repeats step 2 with two other satellites to determine the exact triangulation.

5 CORRECTION
A fourth satellite is used to refine the measurements of the first three and confirm the position.

The conventional GPS system has a margin of error of less than 8.2 ft (2.4 m), although there is also differential GPS, which guarantees precision to within 3.28 ft (.99 m), thanks to the use of a fixed point of reference (see photo) that provides enormous accuracy to the system.

SYNCHRONIZED SIGNALS
The communications center receives the synchronized signals from all the satellites and sends them to the user.

GPS terminals on ships are very similar, in terms of how they look and the technology used, to those that are becoming common in automobiles. What distinguishes them is the software used.

Are There Other "Diabolical Areas" in the World?

The Bermuda Triangle is by no means the only place on earth with a history of disappearing ships and aircraft. Many other oceanic regions, such as the Devil's Sea, have similar notoriety.

Even though the name seen on all maps and nautical charts is the Philippine Sea, the west region of the Pacific situated to the south of Japan is known to the local fishermen by disquieting names such as the Devil's Sea (*Ma no Umi*, in Japanese) or the Dragon's Triangle. Such names result from the numerous and strange disappearances of ships and airplanes from those waters.

This portion of the Pacific is, aside from the Bermuda Triangle, the most referenced of the so-called "Vile Vortices," a series of zones at equal distances from the tropics and that share what seem to be occult powers capable of terrorizing fishermen, mariners and pilots alike.

In the Devil's Sea, just like the Bermuda Triangle, according to investigators there have been dozens of occurrences of disappearing boats and airplanes, encounters with ghost ships, supposed appearances of submarine alien ships and numerous space-time loops, in which airplanes have experienced sudden accelerations in time.

MASSIVE DISAPPEARANCES

Well-versed in the mysterious reputation of the Devil's Sea, investigator Charles Berlitz, widely known for his studies on the Bermuda Triangle, published the book *The Dragon's Triangle* in 1989, in which he claims that five large Japanese Army ships disappeared with more than 700 people on board between 1952 and 1954. According to Berlitz, the Japanese government sent a ship with more than 100 experts to investigate these occurrences, but this ship also disappeared. As a result, authorities decided to classify the area as extremely dangerous.

Investigator Larry Kusche refutes these reports by Berlitz, maintaining that the Japanese government has never declared the area to the south of the archipelago which heads toward open sea as particularly dangerous; that the five missing ships referred to by the specialist in paranormal affairs were, in reality, fishing vessels that were shipwrecked as a result of the multiple storms or tsunamis common in that region, and that the investigation ship Berlitz mentions was actually studying not those disappearances, but the activity of an underwater volcano - Myojin-sho - and the eruption of this volcano sank the ship.

The Vile Vortices

Scottish specialist Ivan T. Sanderson published the article *The Twelve Devil's Graveyards Around the World* in a 1972 issue of *Saga* magazine, in which he outlines his theory of the Vile Vortices; twelve regions – ten situated in locations at equal distances from the Tropics of Cancer and Capricorn and the remaining two at the polar icecaps – in which there are numerous phenomena that are difficult to explain such as those that have caused the disappearances of airplanes and ships, and other paranormal activity. Among these vortices are the Bermuda Triangle and the Devil's Sea, as well as other oceanic zones, such as Easter Island, the Mozambique Channel, and other areas of the Indian, Atlantic and Pacific Oceans. It is surprising that these vortices include areas of land, such as the Indus Valley, the central Sahara and Antarctica.

Twelve Zones of Mystery

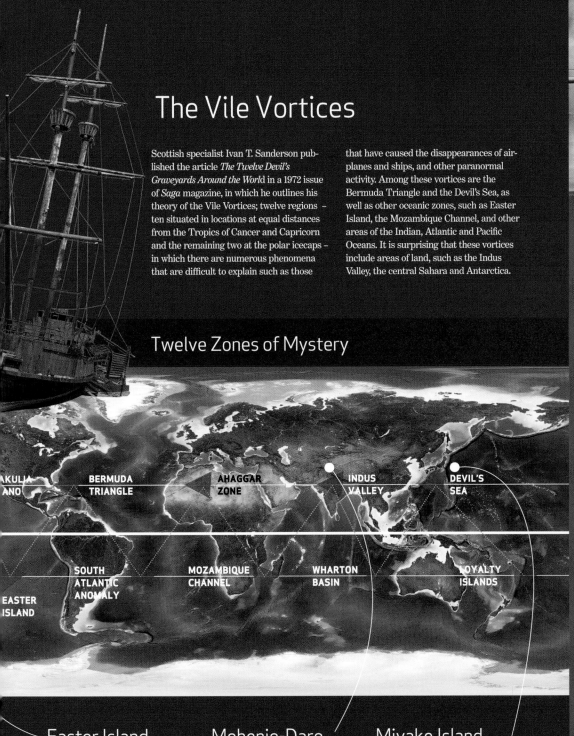

AKULIA ANO

BERMUDA TRIANGLE

AHAGGAR ZONE

INDUS VALLEY

DEVIL'S SEA

SOUTH ATLANTIC ANOMALY

MOZAMBIQUE CHANNEL

WHARTON BASIN

LOYALTY ISLANDS

EASTER ISLAND

The Mystery of Lake Ontario

The approximate area of 95,000 sq mi (246,048 sq km) of this Great Lake is one of the largest masses of fresh water on the planet. Due to its size, the lake has weather patterns similar to those found in the ocean, including storms that have caused a high number of disappearances. Some investigators claim that these occurrences are not due to meteorological causes, and have coined these three mystery zones: the Marysburgh Vortex, situated in the northeast part of Lake Ontario, where two-thirds of the recorded disappearances have taken place; the Sophiasburgh Triangle, just 55 miles (88 km) to the west, where a supposed variation in the magnetic field alters the proper functioning of compasses and causes serious accidents in stormy or foggy weather; and the Lake Michigan Triangle (upper photo), well known after two disappearances: that of a coal freighter in 1937 and that of a Northwest Orient Airlines flight in 1950, which vanished without trace with 58 people on board.

Easter Island
THE GREAT PACIFIC MYSTERY
The more than 600 moai carved from volcanic rock are the well-known face of this enigmatic island situated in the southeast Pacific, about 2,500 miles (4,023 km) off the coast of Chile.

Mohenjo-Daro
A 4,000 YEAR OLD CITY
Located in the center of the vortex at the Indus Valley in Pakistan, the ancient ruins of Mohenjo-daro show the level of civilization that its inhabitants achieved.

Miyake Island
LIVING IN A VOLCANO
Visible from Tokyo and situated in the center of the so-called Dragon's Triangle, Miyake Island is, in fact, a conic volcano whose last eruption was in 1983.

SARGASSO SEA
View from space of this region of the Atlantic Ocean that overlaps part of the Bermuda Triangle. The area is known for the absence of marine currents.

Alternative Hypotheses

Can Anti-gravity Be Achieved on Earth?

In the 1980s, Canadian scientist John Hutchison claimed to have achieved antigravity in his home laboratory in Vancouver by manipulating magnetic fields. Though the experiment was recorded on video, it has never been reproduced. In the experiment, named the Hutchison Effect after its creator, exposing a block of metal to strong magnetic fields supposedly frees the metal object from the effects of gravity. This experiment spawned a series of mutations linking it to the occurrences in the Bermuda Triangle: powerful magnetic fields, the source of compass malfunctions, could lift large ships and planes causing them to disappear. Antigravity is a force equal to that of gravity, but instead of attracting, it repels. Related to antimatter, many respected physicists have described this force based on purely theoretical deductions and believe that anti-gravity can be achieved when extraordinarily high levels of energy are collected, though this is currently impossible to achieve here on earth. When the scientific community accused Hutchison of being unable to repeat the experiment, one of the tenets of scientific method, the Canadian alleged that the military confiscated essential project components in order to protect the discovery, which could be deadly in the hands of terrorists or enemy forces.

JOHN HUTCHISON
The Canadian scientist who supposedly achieved antigravity in his laboratory during the eighties.

Does the Stavenger, Mentioned by Berlitz, Exist?

One of the strongest objections to Charles Berlitz's research of the Bermuda Triangle is the lack of rigor in his documentation. In his book *The Mystery of the Bermuda Triangle: Solved*, Larry Kusche picks apart the disappearances detailed by Berlitz one by one, feeding on his errors and omissions, and finding, for example, strong storms where Berlitz sees only supernatural causes. Probably the most significant case of Berlitz's failure to rigorously document his findings is that of the Stavenger, a Norwegian ship that supposedly disappeared in 1931 in waters off the Bahamas carrying a crew of 43. Kusche could not find a single reference to this disappearance in the press, nor with insurers, nor in the record of maritime accidents. Norwegian authorities indicated that there must be a grammatical error, as no ship called the Stavenger existed, there being records only of ships named Stavanger, in honor of the city bearing the same name, and no ship with that name had disappeared in 1931.

Did the *Freya* Disappear in the Bermuda Triangle?

In his popular essay on the Bermuda Triangle, Charles Berlitz included among the cases he found worthy of analysis the finding of the German ship *Freya* on the high seas, completely abandoned, on October 20, 1902. It has been proven through documentation that the ship was found empty, with some masts down and listing strongly, but the author confuses the city of Manzanillo, on the south side of the island of Cuba and very close to the borders of the Bermuda Triangle, with the Mexican port of the same name, located on the Pacific coast, north of Acapulco. Effectively, the *Freya* shipped out of Manzanillo, Mexico, bound for Punta Arenas, Chile, but was the victim of a fierce tsunami shortly thereafter. That same day all along the Caribbean coast was characterized by total calm, an argument used by Berlitz to place the *Freya*'s disappearance among the mysteries of the Triangle, without realizing that he had located the incident in the wrong ocean!

Was Columbus the Area's First Victim?

In the ship's log from his first journey to America, Genovese sailor Christopher Columbus described a sea replete with seaweed that deceived a crew fearful of running aground and anxious to finally arrive on dry land. He also speaks of magnetic anomalies that confused the compasses, a flash of fire that fell into the ocean, and strange lights boiling in the sea. In later times, this fearful description, logical from a sailor following a path not taken before, was taken out of context and used to buoy the mysterious air surrounding the Sargasso Sea, when it was already known that the seaweed giving it its name accumulated there due to the calms assailing the area, which were often capable of immobilizing a ship, with or without sails. Regarding compasses, Columbus was also one of the first European sailors to experience the noticeable deviation between the geographical North Pole and the magnetic North Pole observed in the western Atlantic. As a result, the compass needle points not to the Polar Star, but some six degrees west.

The flaming streak described by Columbus was most certainly a meteorite crossing the heavens that was lost on the horizon, giving the impression that it landed in the water, while the lights in the sea could well have been the torches of indigenous fishermen working on the shore, as the phenomenon was noted only a few hours before the expedition reached Guanahani Island. Other options include luminescent fish or simple hallucinations due to poor nutrition or the extended length of the journey.

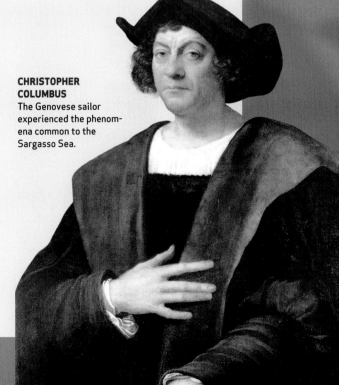

CHRISTOPHER COLUMBUS
The Genovese sailor experienced the phenomena common to the Sargasso Sea.

Does the Full Moon Have an Effect on Shipwrecks?

In his book *The Pyramid Submerged in the Bermuda Triangle*, researcher Marcus Silverman states that most of the disappearances and shipwrecks in the area take place on nights when there is a full moon, and adds that "it is possible that in the profound depths common to the area around the Bahamas, unknown electromagnetic forces, black holes, doors or tunnels lurk that have become similar to an umbilical cord, joining our known reality to another dimension

we ignore." Silverman goes on to defend the theory that the powerful nocturnal light of the full moon could be the astronomical signal that activates the supposed electromagnetic source abandoned by the inhabitants of Atlantis, which alters the function of compasses and causes the confusion and disorientation common to sailors and pilots in the area.

The noticeable influence of the moon on the earth is well-known. The most striking is the moon's effect on the oceans, producing the tides. Another visible effect of the moon is the eclipses, venerated as a divine manifestation among ancient civilizations. However, statistics belie Silverman: the vast majority of the disappearances that have occurred in the Bermuda Triangle, even after eliminating accidents with non-mysterious causes, have not coincided with the full moon. Further, most disappearances for which a time of disappearance has been documented have taken place during the day, when there is more traffic.

FULL MOON
The influence of the earth's satellite on the oceans is noticeable, but does not explain the increased number of accidents.

What Happened to the *Raifuku Maru*?

Bermuda Triangle specialists point out the case of the Japanese cargo ship *Raifuku Maru* as one of the strangest: in April 1925, the ship Homeric received a distress call: "Danger like a dagger! Come quickly! We cannot escape!" Immediately, experts rushed to interpret the significance of the word "dagger": a whirlwind? UFOs? In addition, they spread the idea that the Homeric, upon arriving at the *Raifuku Maru*'s coordinates, found nothing.

In reality, the investigation that followed showed that the Japanese cargo ship had set sail from Boston on a path very distant from the Bermuda Triangle in the midst of a strong storm, and that, hours later, the Homeric received the message, "Now great danger. Come quickly!" in very broken English. Even in the midst of the storm, the Homeric could reach the *Raifuku Maru*'s location, but the stricken ship was already at an angle of 30 degrees and sank before the rescuing crew could react.

Have "Blue Holes" Caused Some of the Disappearances?

Along the coasts of the Bahamas and the Caribbean, as well as in other parts of the world, there are curious formations called blue holes. They are deep, wide, underwater caves with vertical walls carved by the erosion of limestone over thousands of years. They are called blue holes because of their appearance from the air: because of their great depth, the dark blue of the water over the caves contrasts with the turquoise water of the reefs surrounding them. Certain investigations cite the whirlpools that form in the center of the blue holes as the cause of disappearances in the Bahamas. However, despite their mysterious appearance and the black legends surrounding them, the blue holes have been thoroughly explored by biologists and geologists, who admit that strong whirlpools capable of carrying a swimmer or diver to their depths could form in these blue holes, but at most they could pull down small boats, not larger vessels.

Do Giant Beings Exist that Attack Ships?

Legends told by peoples of the sea are replete with stories of giant animals that attack ships. The Kraken, a mythological creature from Norway commonly pictured as a giant octopus or squid who charges ships and devours sailors, is one such legend. Today, the existence of such creatures is known: both the giant squid (genus *Architeuthis*) and colossal squid (*Mesonychoteuthis hamilton*i) are cephalopods that live in the ocean's depths and generally reach lengths of 30 feet (9 m) for males and 45 feet (13 m) for females, though specimens as long as 70 feet (21 m) have been found. These impressive measurements, primarily due to the extraordinary length of their arms and tentacles, places them among the largest animals on earth, second only to the blue whale. Their eyes, up to 10 in (25 cm) in diameter, are without doubt the largest on the planet. These species of giant squid, however, live very far from the coasts, in depths from 1,000 to 3,200 feet (304 to 975 m), and never come to the surface, and as such it has never been possible to capture a living specimen. It is for this reason that stories of attacks on ships by these giant creatures lack any scientific rigor. The fact that these animals were considered legends until just a few decades ago is a clear indication of their aversion to the surface and contact with man.

THE "KRAKEN"
Engraving from 1801 inspired by a supposed attack on a French ship by a giant cephalopod.

To See and Visit

▼ OTHER PLACES OF INTEREST

NATIONAL MUSEUM OF BERMUDA
SANDYS, BERMUDA ISLANDS

In the small parish of Sandys, on the far west side of the archipelago's largest island, is the Bermuda Maritime Museum, a part of the National Museum. The exposition covers five hundred years of sailing history in the military buildings refitted for this purpose next to the pier. Discovered in 1505 by Spanish sailor Juan Bermúdez, from whom the area gets its name, the Bermudas were colonized in the seventeenth century as a result of a shipwreck – a flotilla led by Admiral George Somers – foundered among the islands.

GOLD MUSEUM
BOGOTÁ, COLOMBIA

This museum displays the most complete collection of pre-Hispanic gold work in the world, with more than 34,000 pieces from indigenous Colombian cultures such as the Calima, the Muisca, the Quimbaya, the Tairona, and the Tolima, among others. The most outstanding pieces in this collection include the famous flying ships, small jewels in the shape of planes, created around the year 1000 CE.

NAVAL AIR STATION MUSEUM
FORT LAUDERDALE, FLORIDA

The Naval Air Station at Fort Lauderdale, Florida, is the air base from which the tragically celebrated squadron of Flight 19 took off; the squadron's disappearance in 1945 spurred investigations of the Bermuda Triangle mystery. The air base has an interesting naval air museum, also known by the building housing it, Link Trainer Building #8, which holds documents, books, photographs,

Bahamas

NASSAU
Located on the small island of New Providence, the capital of the Bahamas is a city of 250,000 inhabitants, which is approximately 70% of the archipelago's population. Founded in 1695, Nassau retains its colonial English atmosphere, and has numerous sites of interest related to the sea. The most notable is the Pirate Museum, with recreations of an eighteenth century wharf including a tavern typical of that time and the pirate ship Revenge.

BIMINI
This district, made up of two larger islands, is the closest thing to solid ground in the Bahamas. Apart from the famous "Bimini Road," these islands, North and South Bimini, hide another secret: the source of eternal youth. Although explorer Juan Ponce de León did not find the fountain of eternal youth, in one of the mangrove swamps on North Bimini, a fresh water spring rises up in a natural pool of salt water baptized "The Healing Hole."

THE TONGUE OF THE OCEAN
The Bahamas are an underwater paradise. Just a few hundred yards off the coast of Andros Island lies the so-called "Tongue of the Ocean," an underwater trench reaching 1.1 miles (1.7 km) in depth that is home to an enormous variety of flora and fauna.

Bimini Road

Built by man and later submerged, or simply a capricious natural formation, the Bimini Road never fails to impress. These 2,600 feet (792 m) of aligned rock are found near North Bimini and are easy to access even by inexperienced divers.

artifacts and naval art connected to the area's history, although the most interesting material is certainly that linked to the mystery of Flight 19.

MEL FISHER MARITIME HERITAGE MUSEUM
KEY WEST, FLORIDA
On the island of Key West, south of Florida, stands the Mel Fisher Museum, dedicated to this famous hunter of underwater treasures, famous for his 1985 finding of the wreck of the Spanish galleon *Nuestra Señora de Atocha*, which sank in 1622. Though he died in 1998, Fisher created a foundation with the museum as the centerpiece. The museum houses jewels, coins, and many objects recovered by the diver.

GRAVEYARD OF THE ATLANTIC
CAPE HATTERAS, NORTH CAROLINA
Located on the eastern coast of the state of North Carolina, Cape Hatteras projects outward into the Atlantic, and is one of the key geographical points on the US coast. Hatteras is home to the interesting Graveyard of the Atlantic Museum, which details the cape's history. The cape itself consists of a sandy bank connecting to firmer ground on the coast; this bank has been the site of numerous shipwrecks throughout the ages. The museum contains numerous objects recovered from these shipwrecks and complements a visit to the many ships run aground along the sandy banks.

Glossary

AMPHORA A tall ancient Greek or Roman jar with a narrow neck and two handles.

ARMISTICE An agreement between two opposing sides in a war to suspend fighting; a truce.

ASCETIC Characterized by the practice of severe self-discipline and abstention, usually for religious reasons.

ASTUTE Showing an ability to accurately assess situations or people.

BEDOUIN Arabic-speaking nomadic peoples of the Middle Eastern deserts.

BIFURCATED Divided into two branches or forks.

CANONICAL Included in the list of sacred books officially accepted as genuine.

CELIBACY The state of abstaining from marriage and sexual relations.

CHERUBIM Angelic beings involved in the worship and praise of God.

CODICES Ancient manuscript texts in book form; plural of codex.

CORPORAL Relating to the human body.

CORRODED Destroyed or damaged slowly by chemical action.

DIASPORA A scattered population whose origin lies within a smaller geographic locale or homeland.

ENIGMA Something that is mysterious or difficult to understand.

EPITAPH An inscription on or at a tomb or grave in memory of the person buried there.

ESCHATOLOGICAL A part of theology concerned with the final events of history or the ultimate destiny of humanity, such as the "end time."

ESOTERIC Intended for or likely to be understood by a small number of people with specialized knowledge.

ETHNARCH Political leadership over a common ethnic group or homogenous kingdom.

EXEGESIS A critical explanation or interpretation of a text, especially scriptural.

FRENETIC Fast and energetic in an uncontrolled way.

GNOMON The part of a sundial that casts a shadow.

HERETIC A person holding an opinion or belief that is at odds with what is generally accepted, especially in religion.

HERMETIC A complete and airtight seal.

INCORPOREAL Having no material existence; not made of matter.

MONOTHEISM A belief that there is only one god.

NASCENT Just coming into existence and showing signs of future potential.

OCCULTISM The belief in or study of supernatural powers.

PAGANISM A religion other than one of the main world religions, especially involving nature worship.

PALYNOLOGY The study of pollen grains and other spores, especially in archaeology.

PENSION A regular payment paid to a royal favorite.

PHILOLOGY The study of language in written historical sources.

RESTITUTION Recompense for injury or loss.

RUNIC Consisting of or set down in characters of certain ancient alphabets (runes).

SANCTIFIED Set apart or declared as holy; consecrated.

SEPULCHER A small room or monument of rock or stone in which a dead person is laid.

TALISMAN An object believed to contain certain magical qualities.

THEOCRATIC Related to a political system in which priests rule and derive their authority from a god or gods.

VICTUAL Food or provision intended for consumption.

Further Reading

Barber, Richard. *The Holy Grail: Imagination and Belief.* Cambridge, MA: Harvard University Press, 2004.

Collins, John J. *The Dead Sea Scrolls: A Biography* (Lives of Great Religious Books). Princeton, NJ: Princeton University Press, 2013.

de Wesselow, Thomas. *The Sign: The Shroud of Turin and the Secret of the Resurrection.* New York, NY: Dutton Press, 2012.

Nicolotti, Andrea. Trans. Hiara Olivera. *From the Mandylion of Edessa to the Shroud of Turin: The Metamorphosis and Manipulation of Legend.* Leiden, NL: Brill, 2014.

Parfitt, Tudor. *The Lost Ark of the Covenant: Solving the 2,500 Year Old Mystery of the Fabled Biblical Ark.* New York, NY: HarperCollins, 2009.

Schiffman, Lawrence H., and James Vanderkam, eds. *Encyclopedia of the Dead Sea Scrolls.* Oxford, UK: Oxford University Press, 2000.

Stefon, Matt, ed. *Christianity* (The Britannica Guide to Religion). New York, NY: Britannica Educational Publishing with Rosen Educational Services, 2012.

Vermes, Geza, ed. *The Complete Dead Sea Scrolls in English.* London, UK: Penguin Classics, 2004.

WEBSITES

Ancient Jewish History: The Ark of the Covenant

http://www.jewishvirtuallibrary.org/the-ark-of-the-convenant

The Jewish Virtual Library presents a detailed account of the scriptural basis of the Ark of the Covenant

The Holy Grail

http://d.lib.rochester.edu/camelot/theme/holy-grail

This page from The Camelot Project at the University of Rochester features an archive of texts and images related to the legend of the Holy Grail.

The Orion Virtual Qumran Tour

http://virtualqumran.huji.ac.il

The Hebrew University of Jerusalem offers a virtual tour of the Caves of Qumran, providing photo galleries, videos, and background on the archaeological sites.

Scrolls from the Dead Sea

http://www.loc.gov/exhibits/scrolls

The online exhibit from the Library of Congress on the Dead Sea Scrolls contains images, contextual information, and material details of artifacts, along with a historical overview of the scrolls.

Index